Felted Jewelry

Felted Jewelry
20 STYLISH DESIGNS

CANDIE COOPER

LARK BOOKS
A Division of Sterling Publishing Co., Inc.
New York / London

Editor:
LINDA KOPP

Art Director:
DANA M. IRWIN

Cover Designer:
CHRIS BRYANT

Associate Editor:
SUSAN KIEFFER

Associate Art Director:
LANCE WILLE

Art Production Assistant:
JEFF HAMILTON

Editorial Assistance:
DAWN DILLINGHAM,
DELORES GOSNELL

Illustrator:
ORRIN LUNDGREN

Photographer:
SHERRIE HUNT

The Library of Congress has cataloged the hardcover edition as follows:

Cooper, Candie, 1979-
  Felted jewelry : 20 stylish designs / Candie Cooper.
     p. cm.
  Includes index.
  ISBN 1-57990-870-5 (hardcover)
  1. Felting. 2. Felt work. 3. Jewelry making. I. Title.
  TT849.5.C66 2007
  745.594'2--dc22

                                                    2006028357

10 9 8 7 6 5 4 3 2 1

Published by Lark Books, A Division of Sterling Publishing Co., Inc.
387 Park Avenue South, New York, N.Y. 10016

First Paperback Edition 2010
Text © 2007, Candie Cooper
Photography © 2007, Lark Books, A Division of Sterling Publishing Co., Inc.; unless otherwise specified
Illustrations © 2007, Lark Books, A Division of Sterling Publishing Co., Inc.; unless otherwise specified

Distributed in Canada by Sterling Publishing,
c/o Canadian Manda Group, 165 Dufferin Street
Toronto, Ontario, Canada M6K 3H6

Distributed in the United Kingdom by GMC Distribution Services,
Castle Place, 166 High Street, Lewes, East Sussex, England BN7 1XU

Distributed in Australia by Capricorn Link (Australia) Pty Ltd.,
P.O. Box 704, Windsor, NSW 2756 Australia

If you have questions or comments about this book, please contact:
Lark Books, 67 Broadway, Asheville, NC 28801
(828) 253-0467

Manufactured in China

ISBN 13: 978-1-57990-870-6 (hardcover) 978-1-60059-552-3 (paperback)

For information about custom editions, special sales, premium and corporate
purchases, please contact Sterling Special Sales Department at 800-805-5489
or specialsales@sterlingpub.com.

For information about desk and examination copies available to college and
university professors, requests must be submitted to academic@larkbooks.com.
Our complete policy can be found at www.larkbooks.com.

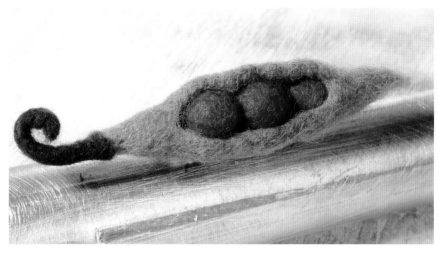

contents

Introduction

I am constantly amazed at the versatility of wool. Through the ages, wool garments have protected man and womankind from the elements. And be it a castle or humble cottage, homes have long been adorned with wool rugs, providing comfort as well as beauty.

Today, just like tubes of paint or skeins of yarn, wool is available in every color imaginable and can also be blended with other fibers to create a wide range of textures and effects. And when wool is felted it becomes a great material from which to make jewelry. Awaiting you in this book are 21 felted earrings, bracelets, earrings, and pins that range in style from contemporary and playful to chic and sophisticated.

Rest reassured that you don't have to be an experienced felt maker or a jeweler to make the projects in this book. If you've never felted before, this book will tell you all you need to know to get started. It's easy to roll simple felt balls and make a small sheet of felt. As you master these basic techniques, you'll become familiar with the material and will learn the different stages that wool travels through to arrive at felt. Knowing this information will give you the confidence to tackle the more advanced projects. And as for jewelry making, you'll learn about the techniques and supplies that will make it easy for you to make any of the projects in this book.

I designed the projects to include a variety of felting techniques, some of which may surprise you! For example, did you know that you could sculpt bubble wrap to make a simple mold to felt on, resulting in a hollow felt form? That's what's used in the Three Peas in a Pod pin on page 106. You can use fabric stiffener and colored pencils to add drawn details to felt, as seen in the Flying Heart Brooch on page 72. There are also dry felting projects, such as the African Sunset

Cuff (page 96), and the Abstract Brooch Trio (page 90), made with a special needle that embellishes wet felted pieces and sculpts the wool, which adds dimension. And who'd think to use a cordless sander to felt wool? Check out the Mixed Media Brooches on page 84 to see what yours truly did with a woodshop tool.

My other goal in designing these projects was to mix the felted wool with other materials—beads, bottle caps, and buttons. Try adding glass or metal beads to your felted pieces; the texture of felt alongside smooth, shiny, or matte surfaces can be rich, and mixing felt with other mediums can lead to fabulous creations! As you gain experience with the felting process, you'll find yourself devising your own methods and embellishments, and in no time you'll be designing your own felted jewelry. In addition to the projects I designed, you'll find jewelry pieces made by talented artists whose work will amaze and inspire you.

Whether you want to add a new craft to your repertoire, or you're already an experienced feltmaker looking for a jewelry project, you've come to the right place. So grab some wool and a bowl of soapy water, and let's get felting!

MATERIALS AND TOOLS

A Few Words about Wool and Felting

Wool is of course essential to making felt, and I will felt with whatever I can get my hands on. Sheep are unique, just like people, and each breed produces its own one-of-a-kind fiber. You will quickly discover that some fibers work better with wet felting, and some better with needle or dry felting due to the fiber's composition.

Wool embarks on quite a journey to get from sheep to the consumer's hands. Shorn wool is called *fleece*, and must be picked through to remove the large bits of dirt and straw. Next, the fleece is washed in very hot water to rid it of all the dirt and oil. This process is handled carefully so as to not accidentally felt it. The fleece is then laid out to dry. At this point the wool is just as it was on the sheep (except it's clean). The little curly or straight pieces

of wool are called *locks*. After it dries, the wool is put through a carding machine, also called a *carder*. The carder combs the fiber out, taking it from separate curly locks to that of a batt or roving form.

A *batt* is a fluffy sheet of wool, and *roving* is a long, organized strand of the combed fibers. You can make felt out of either, but I have found that it's easier to wet-felt with roving because it's easier to lay out evenly.

The felting process hinges on wool's fiber properties. Each fiber has little microscopic scales that open and close. Soap and hot water prompt the opening of the scales. With agitation, pressure, and dish soap (for lubrication and pH factors), the wool's fibers get tangled around each other, and the next thing you know, it has become felt.

When *dry felting* (also called needle felting), the barbs on the felting needles tangle the fibers. In some of the project instructions I tell you the specific sheep breeds I used; however, I encourage experimenting with as many different types of wool as you can get your hands on to learn which ones work best for you and your projects. There are all-natural to rainbow-dyed, super-soft to coarse, and common to exotic wools available on the market. There are also some interesting novelty fibers that you can blend into your wools, such as metallic strands or recycled denim scraps. The possibilities are endless, and I'll warn you, once you begin creating, new ideas will be born quite rapidly.

If you're a beginner, I recommend starting with a user-friendly wool such as Merino for wet felting. This is also the type of wool I used with many of the wet-felted projects in this book. Once you learn the stages the wool travels through during feltmaking, you can begin to experiment with more exotic fibers. I guarantee you will begin to recognize different wools' qualities in terms of what a specific wool may be good for or, conversely, not so good for.

Wet Felting

One of the nice things about feltmaking is that it doesn't require a lot of money to get started. Many of the items required to make felt can be found in your garage or under the kitchen sink. If not, a quick trip to the store will solve that. Once you enter the feltmaking process, you will invent your own useful tools and methods to go with them. Until then, refer to the list of items on the following pages when you begin to felt.

SHANA ASTRACHAN
Pink Felted Ball Ring, 2004
1½ x ⅞ x ⅞ inches
(3.8 x 2.2 x 2.2 cm)
Sterling silver, silk, mohair;
fabricated, wrapped, wet felted
PHOTO BY CHRIS MCCAW

MERJA MARKKULA
Tango, 2006
13 x 7¹/₁₆ x ¹³/₁₆ inches
(33 x 18 x 2 cm)
Wool of Finn sheep,
beads; wet felted
PHOTO BY ARTIST

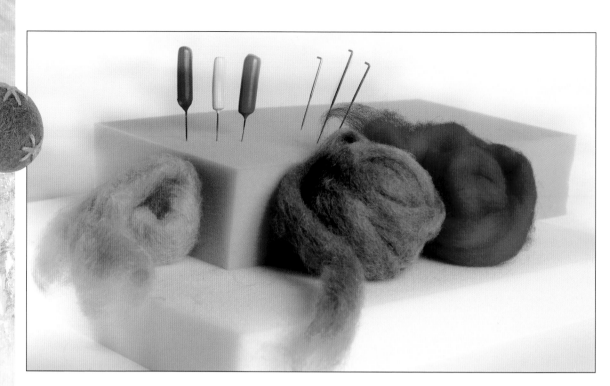

Bubble Wrap

Found in the packing section of office supply stores, a small roll of bubble wrap is ideal when wet felting. Buy the kind that has perforated squares that tear off easily; it works best with the small scale of the felted pieces. Bubble wrap has a slick, bumpy, surface that, when doused with soapy water, is great for agitating and for working a project's edges during the felting process. As you will learn later on, it can be used as a resist, too.

Rubber Car Mat

This is my favorite felting tool. I use a rubber car mat with ridges as the base of my work surface. Mats can be found at mass merchandisers or auto supply stores. The rubber makes it non-skid, and the ridges provide a great agitating surface—making it an all-around useful item.

Forms

Small shampoo bottles (travel-size, or like the ones you get in a hotel), rocks, bubble wrap, and clay forms are just a few items that are useful for three-dimensional felting. Use them as forms to support the wool while you felt, and to help it maintain the general shape. Bubble wrap can be folded and taped like in the Sweet Pea Pin, and then felted around. Clay is a viable option depending on the design and individual needs of your project. You can use clay to make a unique form, but be sure to protect it by wrapping it first in a thin sheet of plastic. Plain plastic bangle bracelets can be felted around and then embellished, as seen in the Mardi Gras Bracelet.

Container

I've been known to use anything from a butter tub to a large bucket to hold hot soapy water when felting. The size of your container will depend on the size of your project. I've found that in general a painter's bucket works nicely.

Sponge

A sponge is useful for gently wetting the wool so as not to disturb the layers. It also comes in handy during cleanup.

Warm Water and Soap

As mentioned earlier, warm water and soap are essential when wet felting. Ask five different feltmakers which soap they prefer, and you are likely to get five different answers. Any transparent liquid dishwashing detergent will work fine. Try to find one that's gentle on your skin.

I like to use a hair color applicator bottle to store my dish soap in. The tapered tip has a small opening, allowing me to dispense just the right amount of soap on the wool. Follow up with a good hand lotion if you choose to use your bare hands while felting.

Rubber gloves

If you're going to be felting for long periods of time, I recommend wearing rubber gloves. My personal preference is to use a pair that has a little texture on the palms and fingers, for agitation purposes.

Hand Towels

It's always nice to have a small stash of hand towels for art use only. Towels are useful before, during, and after feltmaking because felting involves water, and where there's water, there is a need to dry.

Small Scale

A small scale is helpful for weighing out tufts of wool. The use of a scale is especially pertinent when making felt balls for bracelets and earrings, where the tufts need to be of equal weight so they'll be consistent in size after felting.

Small Cordless Sander

A cordless sander speeds up the feltmaking process immensely. Please do not use an electric sander—there is the potential for a shock hazard. I recommend the cordless or battery-operated RYOBI Corner Cat. It's a good choice because hatshapers.com sells special smooth or ridged attachment pieces that fit over the sander, which are geared toward feltmaking.

CAROL CYPHER

A Felted Bead Diva's Lariat, **2004**
47 x 2 x 2 inches
(119.3 x 5 x 5 cm)
Wool, dye, glass lampworked beads, glass seed beads, beading wire; dry felted, strung, bead embroidered
PHOTO BY BOB BARRETT

Dry Felting

Believe it or not, even fewer tools are needed for dry felting (from here on referred to as needle felting) than wet felting.

Fibers for Needle Felting

I mentioned earlier the difference between a wool batt and wool roving. I have used both forms for dry felting. It's not crucial to use one over the other. What is crucial in needle felting is the type of wool you use. Wool fibers that are good for needle felting are coarser than fibers used in wet felting. For the projects in this book, I used wool from the Hampshire breed and from a cross-blend fleece called Wilde. I have also put a top layer of Merino wool over a needle felted core, as seen in the Gold Ring Brooch (page 90). These and other fibers can be purchased on the internet or in some well-stocked fiber and yarn stores. If you're fortunate enough to be able to attend a fiber festival, don't

pass up the opportunity, as they are wonderful places to find unique blends of wool for needle felting. It's also worth mentioning that some needles work better with a certain type of wool versus another. Try different combinations until you find one that is effective.

Felting Needles

Simple to use, *felting needles* are little wires that have sharp points and barbs along the sides. Poking or stabbing at dry wool with a needle is what causes the fibers to felt. Felting needles come in different shapes and numbers, allowing for task versatility, since some will be better for the job than others. If you find that the needle you are using is leaving stab marks, try switching to a different gauged needle. Experimenting and practicing will help you to figure out which numbers work well for what task and which wool types. On the opposite page is a list of felting needles that I used and for what purpose throughout the book.

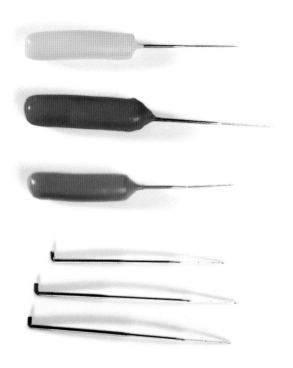

Incorporated Clasp Cord Bracelets, 2006
9 inches (23 cm) long
Natural brown and white wool, silk fabric, natural dyes, semi precious stones, glass seed beads, waxed linen, sewing thread;
wet felted, naturally dyed, hand beaded, stitched
PHOTO BY JOHN LUCAS

A **36-gauge triangle-blade needle** is good for beginning work, such as general sculpting and needle felting wool to a precut shape.

A **38-gauge star-blade needle** is my favorite to work with. It's very versatile in that you can use it to attach yarn or wool to a finished piece, as well as to work the wool in the beginning stages.

A **40-gauge triangle-blade needle** is very fine compared to the first two needles. Due to its small size, this needle is perfect for detail and embellishing work.

Felting needles with special rubberized ends (shown at top of photo above) for easy gripping can be found on the internet. There are even tools that hold more than one needle at a time. Since the projects in this book are small in scale, this tool is not essential to own.

Caution: Felting needles are very sharp and brittle. Please don't leave them where children may find them or where they may get broken.

SHANA ASTRACHAN
Felted Rings, 2003
$7/8$ x $7/8$ x $1/2$ inches each
(2.2 x 2.2 x 1.3 cm)
18-karat gold, sterling silver, silk, mohair; knotted, wrapped, wet felted
PHOTO BY CHRIS MCCAW

Upholstery Foam

Two-to three-inch-thick upholstery foam is the ideal work surface when needle felting because it supports the piece you are working on, while allowing the needles a soft surface on which to land, thus preventing breakage. Inexpensive upholstery foam scraps or chair pads can be found at fabric supply stores. Be aware that over time and with use, the foam will get brittle and will need to be replaced.

Embellishing

Felt surfaces can be embellished as plainly or as intricately as you desire. There are infinite combination possibilities. Fiber and craft stores are great places to seek out interesting materials to add to your felted surfaces. Following are some ideas for embellishing materials.

Fibers

If you choose to use fibers, you can easily wet or needle-felt them into a piece.

- Embroidery threads including metallic, satin, and cotton
- Novelty yarns (i.e., eyelash yarn)
- Metallic or iridescent fibers
- Recycled silk yarn
- Silk hanks
- Raw fibers such as wool, angora, cotton, and locks
- Fabrics or commercial craft felt

PATRICIA SPARK
***June's Necklace*, 1996**
18 x 6 x 2 inches
(45.7 x 15 x 5 cm)
Merino wool, red leather, black lacing, wire, waxed linen; wet felted
PHOTO BY ARTIST
COLLECTION OF JUNE GORCHESTER

Seed Beads

Seed beads and sequins add a bit of sparkle and pizzazz to any felted surface. They come in a range of colors, shapes, and sizes, and can be used one at a time, in multiples, or even stacked on top of another. Seed beads are generally classified by numbers ranging from 15/0 to 1/0—the larger the number, the smaller the bead size.

BARBARA G. KILE
***Bouncing Balls*, 2006**
3 x ¾ x ¾ inches
(7.5 x 1.9 x 1.9 cm)
Wool, sterling silver; wet felted, metal techniques
PHOTO BY MYKE TOMAN

Jewelry-Making Supplies

Transforming your felted pieces into jewelry requires just a few simple materials and hand tools. The tools will be used to manipulate jewelry findings, making it possible to wear your felted pieces. Most of the materials required for each project can be found at your local craft or hobby store. Once there, you will find that the supplies come in a range of quality and prices. Which to choose? The decision is entirely yours. I usually take into consideration why I am making the project and how important it is.

Wire Cutters

Wire cutters are necessary for snipping and cutting head pins, beading wire, and more.

Jewelers Pliers

Round-nose pliers are useful when making loops on the ends of wires.

Flat-nose pliers are used in opening and closing findings and general connections.

Crimping pliers (shown in photo at right) are paired with crimp beads to finish strung pieces of jewelry.

Emery Board

A simple nail file can be used to file the tip of a wire to a point, for ease of stringing felted pieces.

Scissors

Medium to small sharp scissors are used for cutting out felt pieces as well as for trimming threads after stitching.

Needles

A straight upholstery or tapestry needle is a key player when stringing felted pieces. Not only are they strong and sharp, but their eyes are big enough to allow cording to fit through.

Findings

Findings are the small components that are used for the connection and assemblage of jewelry pieces. They generally come in gold and silver.

Some of the findings used in this book are clasps, ear wires and posts, stickpins, hat pins, pin backs, head and eye pins, hair bands, and barrettes.

Adhesives

Adhesives are extremely important in mixed media jewelry because they're what hold the piece to the finding. The following are some adhesives that I have found to work well with wool:

- Two-part epoxy
- Jeweler's cement
- Strong bonding glue

Stringing

In this book you'll see several examples of strung woolen pieces. Sometimes in order to allow the piece to be worn, it must be strung using a material that stretches, such as black beading elastic. This is the case with the African Sunset Cuff. But unless your piece specifically requires using a stretchy material, purchase good quality stringing wire that won't stretch. I've had good luck with memory wire and 49-strand flexible beading wire.

Miscellaneous

The following is a list of additional supplies used in some of the projects.

MIXED MEDIA ITEMS

Keep your eyes open for fun items to incorporate into your felted jewelry designs. These could include bottle caps, buttons, and other found objects. With a bit of imagination and a keen eye, you'll be surprised at the options you'll encounter every day. When choosing your items, keep in mind that they will get wet. For example, watch faces fill up with water and sometimes rust. Paper surfaces will need to be sealed in a plastic laminate.

FABRIC STIFFENER

Use fabric stiffener on felt to hold its shape and change the surface quality from soft to crisp. Look for it in the glue or silk flower section of craft stores.

COLORED PENCILS

Available in every color imaginable, colored pencils allow you to add striking or subtle details to felt pieces. For the best results, spend the money to buy good quality, soft-lead pencils.

TECHNIQUES

How to Wet Felt

It's remarkable that a little agitation, soapy water, and wool make the wonderful material called felt. Have you ever accidentally washed one of your wool sweaters? If you have, you probably noticed it was now too small for you but could possibly fit a child. When washed in hot water, wool shrinks in size anywhere from 33 to 45 percent, depending on the type of wool. When laying out your wool, you must take wool shrinkage into consideration in order to end up with the felted size that you want. For example, Merino wool shrinks to nearly half its size! Here's an easy equation that factors a 33 percent shrinkage, and will help you approximate how big your wool piece will be once it's felted: multiply the number of inches of felted fabric you want by 1.5. For example, if you want 4 inches of felted fabric, multiply 4 x 1.5 (equaling 6). This means that you need 6 square inches of wool to end up with roughly 4 square inches of felt. It's as easy as that.

Splitting Wool Roving into Slivers

Roving is wool that's been washed and then carded (the process of cleaning, separating, and straightening the wool fibers) into long, rope-like lengths.

I like to use combed Merino roving to make sheets of felt or felted coils because of its quick felting qualities and smooth surface appearance. First you must split the roving up widthwise. To do that, place your hand 8 inches from the end of the roving, and pull a length of wool from the roll with the other hand. Then split that piece lengthwise into smaller, thinner pieces called *slivers*. The Priestess Collar Necklace requires splitting the roving widthwise many times. For future reference, one-third width roving refers to Merino roving that has been split into thirds.

Making a Sheet of Felt

The projects in this book require only small sheets of felt no bigger than 4 or 5 square inches in size (photo 1).

1

1 Tear off 10 inches of Merino roving from the ball. Split that length of roving in half. Then tear off small, even length tufts of wool from the two slivers and lay them side by side in the same direction on your rubber work mat, making sure that the edges just barely overlap one another (photo 2).

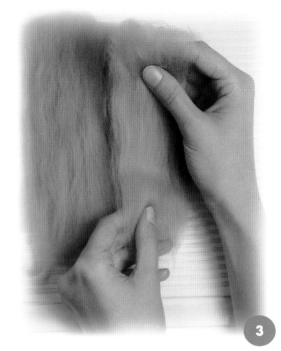

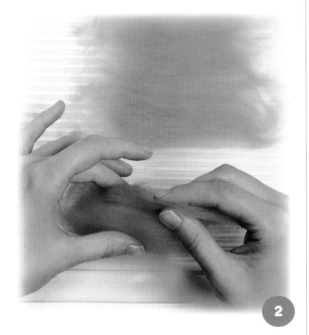

2 Lay the next row on top, perpendicular to the first layer (photo 3). The third layer then must be laid out perpendicular to the second layer. Take care when laying out the wool so that there are no holes. In other words, if you can see the work mat, you have a little more layering to do. The thickness of the felt depends on the number of layers of wool. You'll develop your own style for working in this way; you may tear off thicker pieces or decide to tear off paper-thin pieces. Three to four even layers of wool are a good thickness for the projects in this book, except for the Cubed Bracelet—that project requires that you make a very thick sheet of wool—more like six to eight layers thick. As you practice making felt, you'll learn what works for you, and how thick you want your felt.

3 Note the size of your wool before you begin felting. Later, when you're checking to see if the piece is fully felted, the size will serve as an indicator (because remember, when fully felted, the piece should be roughly one-third or more smaller than when you started).

4 Drizzle some warm soapy water over the layers of wool and add a few drops of dish soap. If you're making felt by hand, make sure your hands are wet and soapy, and begin patting the wool's surface, pushing out bubbles and making sure the wool is totally saturated (photo 4). Lightly use the bottom side of your hands to make small circular motions, taking care not to disturb the layers. This step takes several minutes and patience. A layer of bubble wrap, bubble side down, is also good to use for rubbing.

5 Once the fibers feel like they are strong enough to safely move, turn the piece over and rotate it 90 degrees. You can add more pressure as the piece shrinks and strengthens, but make sure it remains slippery and wet with warm water or else the wool may be more inclined to pill or make what I call "fuzzies" on the surface. Avoid felting the wool in standing water.

6 At this point the fibers should be well intact. If your piece is too soapy, rinse it in some warm water, add soap and continue felting. Now you can begin the *fulling* process, which is simply intense agitation. Fulling is what thickens the felt sheet. Begin by first rolling the piece up, and then roll it back and forth on the rubber work mat (photo 5). Dunk the piece in hot soapy water, and lay it back out on the work mat. Now roll the piece in the opposite direction. Repeat this process for all four sides.

7 You'll know when a piece is fully felted by checking the size (it should be one-third or more smaller overall), and by checking to see if there are any loose layers in between. Do this by trying to pull the sides of the sheet apart (photo 6)—you shouldn't be able to. I look back on some of my earlier pieces and giggle a bit because some are not quite felted all the way. Oops! It happens to all of us. After you've made a few sheets, you'll start to recognize the qualities of finished felt. Once you've confirmed that the piece is fully felted, rinse it in cool water and leave to dry.

Note: When felting a thick sheet of felt versus a thin sheet, the process described above will take considerably longer.

Using a Cordless Sander in Feltmaking

Whenever I need to make a sheet of felt, I use a cordless sander. A sander is a big time-saver, as it agitates the fibers just like when you use your hands, but at a much quicker rate. Due to the potential shock hazard of using an electric sander where water is present, always use a cordless sander. The special washboard felting attachment piece that I mentioned in the Materials and Tools section fits perfectly on a RYOBI Corner Cat cordless sander. After you have laid out the wool, wet it down, and soaped the fibers, you're ready to put the sander to work.

1 Soak up any excess water around your work surface, and place the sander dead-center and directly on top of the wool pile. Depending on the pile's size, in some cases the sander washboard may nearly cover the whole thing.

2 Begin sanding. You don't have to press down too hard for the sander to begin felting the wool. Leave the sander in the middle for a minute or so and then move it over any areas yet to be felted.

3 After the fibers lock into place, pick the sheet up and flip it over, lightly felting the back side.

4 At this point, use the sander like it was an iron, moving it at different angles. Continue felting on both sides, applying increasing pressure, as the piece felts. Once the piece is nearly felted, finish by rolling the sheet up and working it back and forth on the mat, just as if you were making the sheet by hand.

How to Roll a Felt Ball

It takes a little practice to roll a felt ball that is free of wrinkles and lumps. I should also mention that if you're new to felting, start by rolling big felt balls until you get the hang of it. The smaller the felt ball, the harder it is to keep under control. I still have off days where I have to scrap a few attempts at rolling a small felt ball. But don't give up, practice makes perfect here, and this is a great activity to get to know wool and all the stages of felting.

1 Tear off a small piece of wool from the ball. Weigh each piece of wool on a scale if you want consistently sized beads. I use 1 to 2 grams of wool per bead. If I want eight consistent-sized beads, I roll 10 felt balls and pick out the best eight.

2 Lay the piece of wool out flat in front of you. Begin rolling a tight coil/ball shape by tucking the bottom two corners in toward the center and roll it over (photo 7). Continue tucking the sides in as

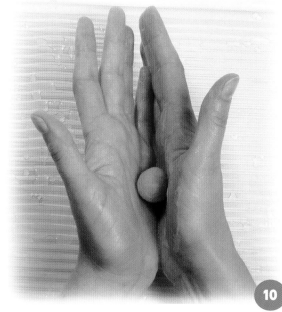

If you need to, add a little soap to your fingers to make them slippery. Continue smoothing the soap over the surface by turning the coil between your fingers. The surface fibers must be locked into place to hold the core shape. This step usually takes approximately two minutes.

you roll, keeping the coil as snug as possible. Grasp the sides of the coil with your middle finger and thumb to keep the coil shape tight.

3 Dip the wool into the bowl of soapy water until it is completely saturated (photo 8). Don't let go of the wool, or it will unwind!

4 Add a small drop of dish soap to the wool and then, with your other hand, smooth the soap over the surface in the same direction that you originally rolled the wool (photo 9). Make sure your fingers slide easily over the wool and that it stays wet.

5 Switch to rolling the ball between your palms (photo 10). At first the ball will feel soft and squishy; be gentle here and don't hurry or add too much pressure. As you continue rolling, it will shrink and harden. One medium-size bead takes approximately 10 minutes from start to finish.

6 Once the ball reaches your desired size and density, rinse it in cold water to remove the soap, reshape it, and then let it dry.

A fun variation of the felt ball is to change the inside and outside colors by rolling up a small tuft of wool into a beginning ball shape, then roll that piece into a new color, and felt. That way if your design calls for cutting the felt ball in half, you will see two colors. Using this technique, you can create a rainbow of layers by rolling several different colors around a ball.

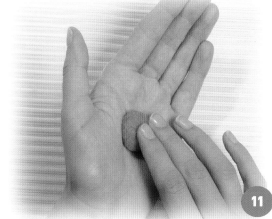

Making Various Bead Shapes from a Ball

You can alter the shape of a felt ball by simply chang-ing the final felting motions and sculpting the bead into a new shape. Ovals, rounded cubes, flat round beads, and more can be created by changing how you felt the final form. Think of how you might roll a ball of clay and how you would change the shape of it into a new shape; most of the time this theory can apply to felting. After you rinse the piece in water to remove the soap, reshape it and leave to dry.

FLAT & ROUNDED

1 One variation of the round felt ball is a flat round bead. To make a flat bead, begin as you would to make a round felt ball. After you roll the felt ball between your palms for a couple of minutes (the ball should still be squishy), you'll form the ball into the shape you want it to be.

2 In this case, sandwich the ball in between your slightly rounded palms and felt, using small circular motions with your fingers on the other hand (photo 11).

CUBE-SHAPED

Pinching the sides of the felt ball between both hands' index fingers and thumbs can make a cube shape (photo 12). Keep track of where you pinch,

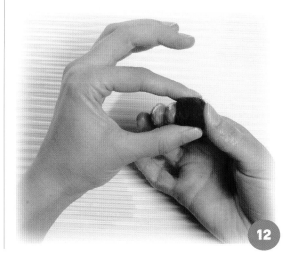

and rub each side of the cube back and forth on bubble wrap. Rinse the ball in cool water, reshape, and leave to dry.

LONG AND OVAL

1 For a long oval bead, as seen in the African Sunset Cuff, start by rolling the roving as you would to make a felt ball. The middle thickness of the bead will depend on how much you roll up initially.

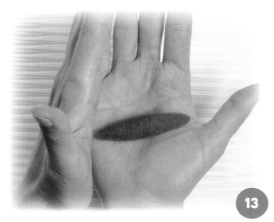

2 When you're happy with the middle thickness, continue rolling straight forward with the roving, making the overall shape more like a tube.

3 Hold the shape and saturate it thoroughly with warm soapy water. Put a little dish soap on your palms and the felt piece, and make short back-and-forth motions with your hands, with the piece nestled in the crease of your palms (photo 13). Check the piece often, and if the sides are getting too long, gently scoot them back toward the center.

4 Once the bead is shrinking and getting tighter, you can switch to rolling it on your work mat (photo 14). A variation of this is to make the ends rounded by working the end of the shape down in your cupped palm.

Making a Flower from a Sheet of Felt

You'll need 2 to 3 grams of wool to make a flower with a finished size of approximately 3 inches in diameter.

1 Lay out two layers of roving, forming an approximate 4½-to 5-inch square, just like you were making a sheet of felt. Try to keep the corners more rounded than square by tucking them under slightly (photo 15).

2 Place your hand on top of the stack of wool and use a sponge to gently wet the layers, being careful not to disturb the wool pile (photo 16).

3 Add a drop of soap, a layer of bubble wrap (bubble side down), and then use a sander to felt the piece (photo 17), referring back to Using a Cordless Sander in Feltmaking, if necessary. Once the layers are holding together, it's safe to pick the piece up. Remove the bubble wrap and sand directly on the wool, turning the piece 90 degrees, and working on both sides.

4 When the piece is nearly felted, find the center of the "flower" and place it on the tip of your index finger, gathering and pulling the sides of the piece down around your finger like a closed umbrella (photo 18). Remove the piece from your finger, and keeping it in the umbrella shape, roll it on your work mat or in between your palms. At this stage you're coaxing it into a flower shape.

5 You can work the sides and edges of the flower by laying the piece on bubble wrap and, with your three middle fingers inside, working the piece by sliding it back and forth, rotating it as you go (photo 19). You can make a ripple-like edge on the petal by placing your index finger on the edge of the flower and sliding it back and forth on bubble wrap. This action will pull that edge of wool in toward the center. Skip a little space and repeat for the remainder of the edge. Alternate felting the flower on the bubble wrap and rolling the umbrella shape until the layers are fully felted, and you're satisfied with the final shape. You can also trim the edge of the flower with scissors for a more crisp and controlled edge. Thoroughly rinse the flower in cool water, reshape and leave to dry.

Felting a Coil

Coils are fast and easy to make. Use them in your projects as is or chop them up into pieces to make beads. A felt coil can be rolled as thick as a garden hose (or thicker) or as thin as a piece of yarn. They are rolled much in the same way as you would roll a piece of clay to make a "snake." To roll a coil, tear off the desired length of roving from the ball.

1 If you aren't sure how thick you want the coil, test it by holding the sliver with both hands and twisting it in opposite directions (photo 20). When the sliver has no more fluff and looks solid, this is a rough indication of how thick it will be once it's felted. We'll call this the twist test. Too thick? The roving can easily be split into thinner pieces by holding on each end and pulling the length apart. You can repeat this as many times as you like until you reach your desired size.

2 Dip the sliver in warm soapy water, and lay it out on your work mat. Add a drop of soap to your fingers and roll the piece back and forth on the mat (photo 21). Wearing rubber gloves will save your hands from feeling like they've been put through the wringer, and if the gloves have grips they will speed the felting process. In between rolling the coil on the mat, you can scrunch and swish it around in the water. It takes approximately five to seven minutes to roll a medium-size coil.

Using Forms

Materials such as bubble wrap, bottles, and rocks are examples of items that can be used as forms, allowing you to create unique felted shapes. Basically anything that maintains its shape when wet can be used as a form. The Three Peas in a Pod brooch, Chic Rosebud Hatpin, and Mardi Gras Bangle bracelet's shapes were all created by using a form while being felted. Although each project has specific felting elements, the following information describes the basic principals of using a form in felting.

1 Simply wrap one to three layers of slivers over the top of a form, keeping the wool snug (photo 22). You can also dip the slivers in warm soapy water first, and then wrap them around the form. Either way, take care not to twist the fibers as you're wrapping. You can make the inside of a felted piece a different color from the outside by wrapping the form with the inside wool color first, and following on top with a different color.

2 Hold the wool in place with one hand, and dunk it down into the warm soapy water until it's fully saturated.

3 With the other hand, add a few drops of soap to the surface (photo 23).

4 Smooth the soap over the wool in the same direction as you wrapped it (photo 24). Keep the piece wet and continue to smooth over the surface with your fingers, tucking the wool back into place if it slips off the form.

5 Once the felted surface feels secure, add more pressure by rolling the felted piece (while still on the form) on the work mat (photo 25).

Tip: You can also take a piece of bubble wrap and wrap it around the form, rubbing it vigorously against the felt (photo 26).

6 If you're able, remove the piece from the form and gently felt the inside of the shape with your fingers. Roll the piece back and forth on the work mat in the same orientation as it was on the form (photo 27). Stretch the piece back over the form if it gets too small. Once you're finished felting, rinse the piece and leave it to dry.

How to Needle Felt

Needle felting is rewarding because it's fast and easy. Plus you have added control by using the needle. Needle felting is also more forgiving, in that if you felt a piece of wool into your main piece and you don't like it, no worries; just pull the piece of roving or wool you were felting off the piece and try again.

Freeform Needle Felting

Set your block of upholstery foam on your work surface. Some people like to place the block on their lap, but if you do, make sure the block of foam is thick enough to avoid getting stabbed in the thigh.

Tear off small tufts of wool and begin to poke and stab it with the felting needle (photo 28). Sounds aggressive, I know, but the results are amazing. Remember that different needles work better with some types of wool than others, so it's a good idea to have different numbers of felting needles on hand. You can roll, fold, and twist the wool over itself and continue poking to build up thickness.

28

Tip: New colors can be worked in the same way (photo 29). Whichever angle you stab is what direction the wool will go. An example would be if the "V" at the top of a heart shape weren't defined enough, you'd poke the needle into the bottom inside of the "V" to add more definition. Poking the needle in a skimming fashion across the surface in all different directions can tighten the surface layers of wool.

29

Needle Felting onto a Base Felt Shape

You can needle-felt wool onto other pieces of fabric and felt. Some of the projects in this book call for tracing a pattern and transferring it onto a piece of acrylic/polyester craft felt. Craft felt is sold as inexpensive sheets in the craft and fabric stores. The polyester felt shape makes it easier to create specific shapes such as a butterfly because you have a guide to felt on.

1 Place a polyester felt shape on top of your foam block, and lay out tufts of wool that roughly fit into the shape.

2 Begin poking the wool into the shape, making an even covering (photo 30). Continue building up a thick layer of wool; don't forget a thin layer on the back side to cover the felt shape. If the sides don't look round enough, tack some wool on the front and bring the opposite end around to the back, and felt it in.

3 You may notice that the felting needle left some small holes in the surface of your piece. Or maybe you just want the overall look of the shape to be smoother and the fibers tighter. Have no fear, it's safe to wet felt it. Dip the shape in soapy water, add a little soap to your fingers, and gently rub it on the bubble side of some bubble wrap. You can also work the inside and outside of the piece with your fingers to add definition to the shape. Rinse the piece in cool water to remove all the soap, and towel dry. Form the piece back into shape, and let it dry.

Caution: Don't take your eyes off what's going on in front of you, and keep your fingers out of the path of a felting needle. Store your needles in a safe place and away from children. I said it before, and I'll say it again, these things are sharp and painful when they come in contact with skin!

Felting a Sweater

Wool sweaters from thrift stores can be felted (also called "fulled") in a jiffy. Check the label on the garment and make sure it's 100 percent wool, because it will not felt nicely if there are any synthetic fibers or cotton blended with the wool. I especially like looking for sweaters with ribbed textures or raised patterns.

To felt a sweater, set your washing machine to small load on hot, add a dash of laundry soap and the sweater, shut the lid, and walk away. Be aware that fulling sweaters creates a lot of lint and fuzz balls in the washer and may not be the friendliest way to treat your appliance, so consider placing the sweater in a zippered pillow protector or lingerie bag. When the washer is finished, you can check to make sure the sweater is completely felted by making a small cut with scissors and checking to see if the threads unravel. If they are still loose, repeat the wash.

The textured leaves on this flower were cut from a felted sweater.

Surface Embellishing

There are endless possibilities and combinations when it comes to decorating felt surfaces. Fabrics, threads, sequins, novelty fibers, and beads are just a few to try. I guarantee that once you begin felting, you will concoct your own unique ideas, but here are a few to get you started.

Using Embroidery Stitches

Embroidery stitches can create fantastic additions to your felted work. Simple stitching can produce fun surfaces that appear as if they have been doodled on. And there are elaborate stitches that lend a sophisticated look. Using different types of threads such as pearl cotton or metallic can add a lot of character to your work as well. Strands of embroidery floss can be divided or used as is when you buy it. I recommend checking out some embroidery stitch books because there are so many interesting stitches to try. Whichever stitch you choose to use for a project, practice a few stitches on a scrap surface before jumping into the actual piece. It's no fun to rip out stitches and risk damaging the felt surface.

When embroidering, don't tug too hard on the needle end. I say this because depending on which types of wool you use, felt sometimes has a porous surface; and if you pull too hard, small stitches can get lost, and long stitches lose length. Pull just enough so the stitches sit on top of the surface—not too loose, not too tight.

Anchoring the Thread

Before you can begin sewing and embellishing onto the felt surface, you must first anchor the thread. Thread the needle with the desired thread and secure it to the felt surface by taking two forward stitches and one back stitch. If you are embellishing a felt sheet, you can easily anchor on the back side of the fabric. Anchoring to a felt ball is a little trickier, but with careful planning, you can find a discreet spot and possibly cover it with a bead or stitch later if it shows.

RUNNING STITCH

A straight stitch is a single stitch, and you can use it in multiple ways. Simply anchor the thread and begin passing the needle in and out of the felt. A running stitch is another form of the straight stitch except it makes a dashed line. Many of us learned the words, "over, under, over, under" when we were learning to sew. The stitch is done just how it sounds.

1 Bring the needle up at A.

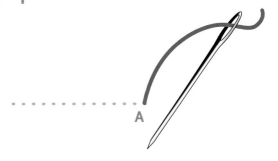

2 Working right to left, bring the needle in at B and out at C, making a small stitch along the stitching line.

3 Make another stitch the same length as the first. Repeat until you reach the desired length.

Asterisks and Xs can also be made with the straight stitch. Try variations like zigzagging the stitch or mixing two or three different kinds of stitches. How about adding some beads within the stitches?

CHAIN STITCH

A chain stitch is an embroidery stitch where the stitches look like a chain when complete.

1 To make a basic chain stitch, anchor your thread and then put the needle back down at the same spot you started so that there is a loop on top of the surface. Holding the loop with your finger, bring the needle down.

2 Bring the needle up through the loop on the stitching line at A. (Make sure the thread is under the needle.) Pull the thread gently to tighten the loop.

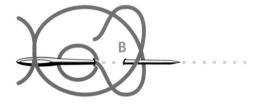

3 Bring the needle up at B, taking care to insert where the thread emerged in the previous loop.

4 Repeat. Make a vertical stitch to finish the loop. Keep repeating this sequence, creating a chain.

There are many variations on the chain stitch, but let me explain the lazy daisy stitch.

LAZY DAISY

The lazy daisy stitch, shown on page 34, is very similar to the basic chain except the stitch is separate and by itself versus connected to the rest of the stitches. The name indicates what it's often used for, and that's for making stitches that look like flower petals.

Gallery

CAROL CYPHER
A Lariat for Georgia, **2006**
30 x 6 x 5 inches
(76.2 x 15 x 12.5 cm)
Wool, dye, glass seed beads; wet felted, bead embroidered
PHOTO BY BOB BARRETT

LISA KLAKULAK
Squash Blossom Ring, **2006**
Stands 1 ½ inches (3.8 cm)
off finger
Wool, natural dyes of osage bark and indigo, madder and cochineal, glass seed beads, black onyx cabochon, tourmaline spheres, waxed linen, sewing thread; wet felted, hand beaded, stitched
PHOTO BY JOHN LUCAS

1 Bring the needle up at A and insert it as close as possible to A, forming a loop. Bring the needle up through the loop on the stitching line at B. (Make sure that the thread is under the needle.)

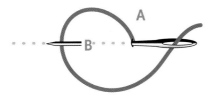

2 Make a vertical stitch to secure the loop. This stitch may be tiny or long.

3 Poke the needle through to wherever you want the next petal.

FRENCH KNOT

A French knot is a small, knotted stitch that sits on top of the surface much like a seed bead. French knots add a new texture to a felt surface depending on how closely you space them.

1 Bring the needle up at A.

2 Hold the thread taut between the index finger and thumb of your nonstitching hand and twist the needle around the thread twice. (If you prefer a fine knot, twist the thread around the needle once.)

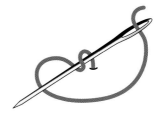

3 Insert the needle halfway at B (right next to A) and slide the twist down the needle so that it lies on the fabric. Slowly push the needle through. Don't let go of the wrapped thread end until you have pulled the needle through and removed all the slack, resulting in a secure stitch.

WHIPSTITCH

In this book a whipstitch is used to stitch small felt pieces to a larger felt piece, holding them in place. It also serves as a decorative edge to the work.

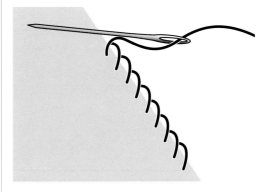

1 Anchor the thread on the back of the piece and bring the needle up through the small felt piece.

2 Poke the needle back down through the middle of the large felt base and up through the small piece, just down from where the last stitch started. This creates a little gap between the stitches.

3 Repeat this stitch around the border of the small piece and then anchor the thread on the back again.

Seed Beads and Sequins

1 First check to make sure the needle you plan to use fits through the hole in the bead or sequin. Thread one bead over the needle and onto the thread, then put the needle back down into nearly the same place as where you started.

2 Angle the needle so it comes up through where you want to place your next bead. For sequins, string one sequin followed by a seed bead, and then thread the needle back through the hole in the sequin so that the seed bead holds the sequin in place.

3 Anchor the thread as you did when you started, and trim the end.

Appliqué

Other fabric pieces can be stitched onto felt surfaces with the straight stitch. Small circles from wool or a cotton print can be stitched on with an outline or by taking small, hidden stitches and turning the edges of the fabric under.

Stiffening Felt

Why not change the surface quality of the wool with fabric stiffener? Fabric stiffener can be found in craft and fabric stores and is used to stiffen silk flowers, fabrics, and, in this case, felt. Use scraps of wool to test out the fabric stiffener first to make sure you like the effect. You can spray it on the wool and repeat if needed. To make it extra stiff, dip the felt piece in the solution and pat away any excess with paper towels. Lay it out on plastic to dry. Repeat if necessary. When I plan on using colored pencils to embellish a piece of

Gallery

KRISTIN LORA
Felt Ball Grid Pin,
2006
3 x 3 x ¾ inches
(7.5 x 7.5 x 1.9 cm)
Fine silver,
felt balls;
hand fabricated,
handmade
PHOTO BY
SARA STATHAS

SHANA ASTRACHAN
Black Felted Ring, 2003
⅞ x ⅞ x ½ inches
(2.2 x 2.2 x 1.3 cm)
18-karat gold, sterling silver, silk, mohair; knotted, wrapped, wet felted
PHOTO BY CHRIS MCCAW

felt, I use the dip method. Some fabric stiffeners can be strong smelling and should be used in an area with good ventilation. Be sure to wear rubber gloves to protect your hands when working with any sort of chemical solution.

Colored Pencils

Extra-stiff wool can be further embellished with acrylic paints, paint pens, or even soft-lead colored pencils. I prefer extra stiff Merino wool when working with colored pencils. Experimenting on scraps is pertinent here in order to find out what works best with your wool and style. I generally don't use these techniques if the piece will be laying on bare skin. Brooches or earrings are good candidates instead.

Using a Felting Needle

There are a couple of things to take into consideration before grabbing a felting needle and getting busy adding a design.

Felt balls require a little care when needle felting embellishments onto them. If you're planning a specific design such as wool stripes, then don't completely wet felt the object that you want to needle felt. Instead, felt it approximately three-quarters of the way, leaving it a little soft and squishy to ease the needle-felting process and to avoid a lot of broken needles. Felting needles are very brittle and can snap easily when felting a design into a hard felt ball. The piece should be

totally dry when you needle-felt on it. Once the design is in place, then you can finish it by wet felting. On the other hand, wet felting can alter the appearance of the needle-felted design, so if you want it to stay exactly the same, then you must fully felt the piece and then needle felt.

To avoid a pile of broken needles, try to insert the needle into a place and bring it back out as straight as it went in. It's when you pull the needle out at a different angle that it snaps.

Another thing to take note of is that certain felting needles will be better suited for the job than others, but you'll just have to experiment to see what works best with what. For example, I like to needle-felt eyelash yarn into felt balls, and have found that a 40-gauge needle works better for this than a thicker needle. It takes a little patience to needle-felt onto a felted surface, but the results can be really interesting. I have had success with needle-felting locks, recycled silk, novelty yarns, and other wools into felt balls and sheets. Some materials take a little more effort than others, as you will find.

Mixing Wool Colors and Textures

Mixing wool colors and adding novelty yarns is a great way to add interest to your work. Enjoy experimenting and exploring the many possibilities of new surfaces in your own work with the following information.

Making a Cobweb Layer

If you're a fan of cobweb Halloween decorations, you'll be a pro at what I'm about to explain. You know the white cobwebs you can buy at Halloween to string across your windows and doorways? You have to pull and tug them apart to make them look like a cobweb. The same goes for wool roving when making a cobweb layer.

SHANA ASTRACHAN
Stacking 'O' Rings, 2005
1½ x ⅞ x ½ inches
(3.8 x 2.2 x 1.3 cm)
Sterling silver, wool;
fabricated, wet felted
PHOTO BY CHRIS MCCAW

Tear off a piece of roving and begin to gently pull it apart, taking care to leave strands connected in all directions. Pull the piece from many angles. You can now lay this piece on top of the wool tufts laid out for a sheet of felt (photo 31). A cobweb layer is also useful for acting as a net to hold shapes (such as small tufts of roving twirled up to make polka dots) or novelty fibers in place while you felt. Make one in a different color or, for a more camouflaged net, use the same color as the majority of a sheet. You can double or triple layer cobwebs too.

Incorporating Novelty Fibers

Novelty fibers such as the beautiful textured yarns, silks, laces, and metallic strands found at special fiber shops can be laid on the surface of unfelted wool sheets. As you felt, the wool will shrink and tangle around the fibers, creating a lovely and unique effect. You can tease out some of the fibers to make more openings for the wool to latch on to.

Other abstract things to felt into your surfaces are straw, wires, and plastic pieces. A cobweb layer can be useful for holding them in place as you felt.

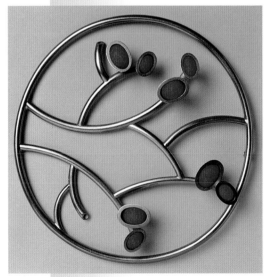

DOROTHY HOGG
*Brooch in the
Artery Series*, 2003
4¼ inches (11 cm)
Silver, red felt; oxidized
PHOTO BY JOHN K.
MCGREGOR
IN THE COLLECTION OF
ABERDETH MUSEUM AND
ART GALLERY

Blending the Wool

1 Small amounts of two different colors of wool can be blended easily by hand. Tear off two 6-inch lengths of wool, and lay them on top of each other (photo 32).

2 Grab each end with both hands and pull apart (photo 33). Lay those two pieces on top of each other and repeat.

3 Repeat Step 2 until you are happy with the total blend (photo 34).

Turning Felt Pieces into Jewelry

Once you've created an assortment of felt beads, coils, and flowers, you'll want to transform them into jewelry to show them off. With just a few simple jewelry-making techniques, you'll be adorned in felt in no time!

Stringing Felt Pieces

Felt can be strung onto a wide variety of cords and wires. The following will explain a few tips and tricks to help you easily string your felt pieces.

1 The majority of the time I use a large tapestry or upholstery needle and 49-strand flexible beading wire to string felt balls and other pieces because it is strong and easy to pull through the felt. Make a kink approximately 1 inch in from the end of the wire. This is where the needle will sit.

2 Slide or twist a felt piece carefully onto the needle. I sometimes encounter difficulty getting the felt piece over the stringing material and eye of the needle, so I use flat-nose pliers to grasp the tip of the needle and pull it through (photo 35). If you do this, point the needle in a downward position toward your work surface so as not to hurt anything or anyone. If you want to add glass beads in between the pieces, you must remove the needle and then put it back on when you're ready to resume stringing felt.

Note: The projects in this book do not require the need for an awl. If your stringing material is thicker than beading wire (i.e., suede lace), you can use an awl to carefully poke a hole in the felt piece. Please be careful; an awl is a sharp tool.

Using Head and Eye Pins

Felt pieces can be strung onto wires such as head pins and eye pins, too.

1 Simply cut the end of the wire at an angle so there's a sharp tip to poke through the wool.

2 Support the end of the wire between your thumb and index finger so that when you twist and slide the felt piece on, it doesn't bend the wire. If cutting it at an angle with wire cutters doesn't work, you can also file a sharp point onto the tip of the wire using an emery board or a small file.

Making a Loop

A loop can be made at the end of head pin or eye pin wires by using your flat-nose pliers to make a 90-degree bend in the wire just above the felt piece (photo 36). The first time I attempted to make a loop at the end of a wire with a felt ball on it, I mistakenly squished the felt ball down as I was making the bend. After I let go and the felt ball stretched back out, there wasn't enough space so it looked more squashed than round. Trim the wire to a ⅜-inch length (or longer depending on desired loop size), and make a loop with the round-nose pliers by rolling the end around.

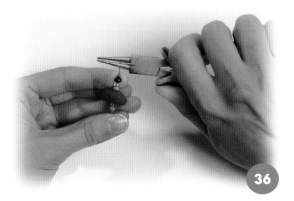

36

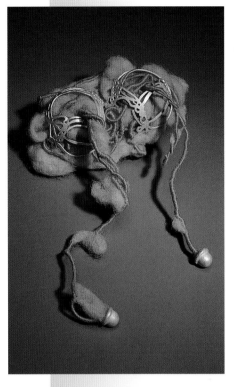

ANDREA WAGNER
Wonderbliss, **2001**
7½ x 6¼ x 1¼ inches
(19 x 16 x 3 cm)
Silver, wool, dye, thread; wet felted, hand dyed, hand stitched, metal casting, metal sheet construction, solder
PHOTO BY CLAUDE CROMMELIN
PRIVATE COLLECTION

CAROL CYPHER
Untitled, **2006**
22 x 3 x ¾ inches
(55.8 x 7.5 x 1.9 cm)
Wool, dye, vintage glass beads, beading wire, magnetic closure; wet felted, strung
PHOTO BY BOB BARRETT

Using Crimp Beads

Crimp beads can be used to secure the findings, such as clasps, in place.

1 String the final bead, the crimp bead, and the clasp onto the end of the beading wire, and put the tail of the wire back through the crimp bead.

2 Spread the two wires out on opposite sides of the crimp bead, and use the notched setting on the crimping pliers to start the crimp, creating a U shape (photo 37).

3 Turn the crimp 90-degrees and crimp with the rounded notch on the crimping pliers, folding the crimp bead over. Remove excess slack between beads and repeat for the opposite end.

Connecting Jump Rings

A jump ring is a simple way to connect a beaded head pin to a necklace or other finding. In order to keep the jump ring's shape, be it oval or round, it must be opened properly using two pairs of pliers. A common mistake is to open the jump ring by pulling the two ends apart, but this leads to frustration when it comes time to close the ring because now it is misshapen.

Instead, open the ring by clamping the pairs of pliers on either side of the opening and twisting, so that one side of the ring comes toward you and the other away from you (photo 38). Open the loop at the end of an eye pin in the same fashion.

Attaching Pin Backs

Have you ever seen a pin being worn that looks as if it is going to take a nosedive onto the floor? That could be due to a mechanical problem. Look at the back of your piece and find the horizontal centerline. Now find the center of that upper section and attach your pin back here, where the majority of the weight will then hang from the pin back. Most pin back findings have holes along the bar. Anchor your thread and then secure the pin back in place with three stitches through each hole. Using a curved needle is helpful for more rigid surfaces such as the Mixed Media Brooches.

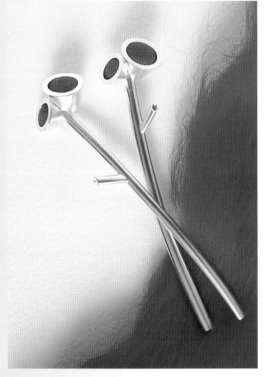

DOROTHY HOGG

Brooch in the Artery Series, 2003
4 x 2 x ⅝ inches
(10.5 x 5 x 1.5 cm)
Silver, red felt
PHOTO BY JOHN K. MCGREGOR

RHONDA WYMAN

Narnia Ring, 2004
½ x ¾ inches
(1.3 x 1.9 cm), size 6
Sterling silver, wool felt; pierce
and saw, hand form, tension
set
PHOTO BY MARTY DOYLE

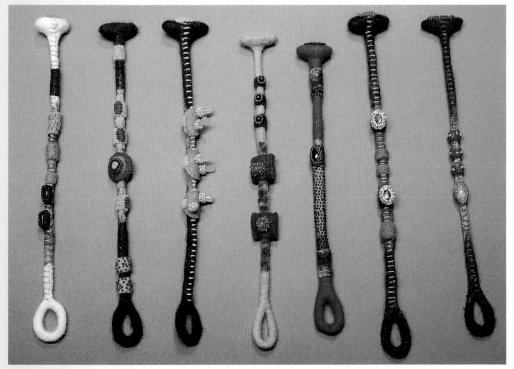

LISA KLAKULAK

Incorporated Clasp Cord Bracelets, 2006
9 inches (22.5 cm) long
Natural brown and white wool, silk
fabric, natural dyes, semi precious
stones, glass seed beads, waxed linen,
sewing thread; wet felted, naturally
dyed, hand beaded, stitched
PHOTO BY JOHN LUCAS

Gallery

LEXI ROJAHN

Ladyslipper Orchid Pin, 2006
3¼ x 3½ x 1½ inches
(8.2 x 8.8 x 3.8 cm)
Wool, beads, thread, silk cocoon, silk; wet felted,
machine free stitched, hand sewn, hand beaded,
cut
PHOTO BY MARCIA ALBERT

LORI FLOOD

Five Felt Pendants, 2006
3 x 18 x 3 inches (7.5 x 45.7 x 7.5 cm)
Dyed wool, loops, sliders, wire; wet felted,
needle felted, strung
PHOTO BY TOM McCOLLEY

Felted Jewelry

MIRIAM VERBEEK

Wings, 2006
13 x 10 x 5½ inches
(33 x 26 x 14 cm)
Wool, silk; wet felted
PHOTO BY ARTIST
PRIVATE COLLECTION

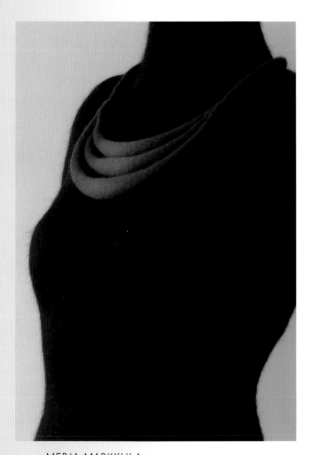

MERJA MARKKULA

Celebrated, 2006
10½ x 7 x ½ inches
(27 x 18 x 1.5 cm)
Wool of Finn sheep; dyed, wet felted
PHOTO BY ARTIST

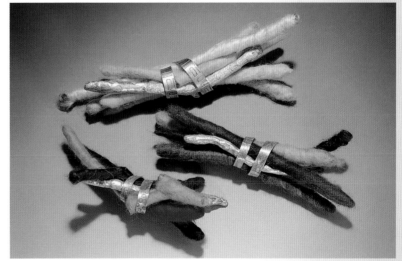

BARBARA G. KILE

Stick Pins, 2004
1 x 5 x 1 inches (2.5 x 12.5 x 2.5 cm)
Twigs, wool, PMC, sterling silver; wet felted, etched, metal formed, soldered
PHOTO BY JACK ZILKER

Gallery

BRIGIT DAAMEN

Boa-necklace, 2004
1³/₄ x 2 x 45 inches
(4.5 x 5 x 115 cm)
Diverse hat felt, rubber, thread; felt
deformed over handmade moulds, rubber
layer added, hand stitched
PHOTO BY ARTIST

LEBRIE RICH

Flower Pins, 2006
4 x 4 inches
(10 x 10 cm)
Wool, acid dye, metal clip; wet
felted, hand constructed
PHOTO BY JOHNATHON ALLEN

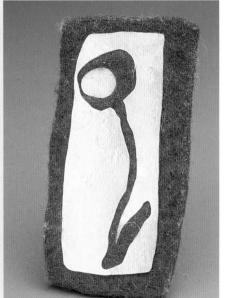

RHONDA WYMAN

Garden Brooch, 2004
18k yellow gold, wool felt;
forged, riveted
PHOTO BY MARTY DOYLE

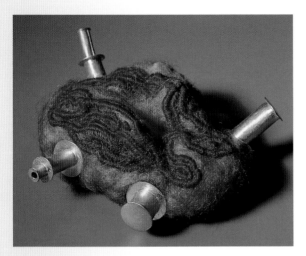

ANDREA WAGNER

Pose, 2001
2 x 1¾ x 1 inches
(5 x 4.5 x 2.5 cm)
Gold, wool, dye, thread; wet felted, hand dyed,
hand stitched, metal sheet construction,
soldering
PHOTO BY CLAUDE CROMMELIN

LIZ CLAY

Flower Collar, 2006
14 x 12 inches
(36 x 30 cm)
Wool, silk, glass beads; wet felted, finished with dry felting,
hand stitched beads
PHOTO BY STUDIO 1

KRISTIN LORA

Felt Ball Cufflinks, 2006
1 x 1 x 1 inches (2.5 x 2.5 x 2.5 cm)
Silver cufflinks, handmade felt balls; hand
fabricated, oxidized
PHOTO BY SARA STATHAS

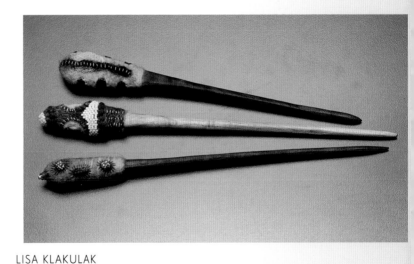

LISA KLAKULAK

Grouping of Hairsticks, 2005
7 inches (17.5 cm) long
Wool, naturally dyed fleece, wood sticks, glass seed beads, waxed
linen, sewing thread; wet felted, hand beaded, stitched
PHOTO BY JOHN LUCAS

Gallery

LISA KLAKULAK

Stone Pendant, 2005
9 x 5½ inches
(22.5 x 13.8 cm)
Wool, silk fabric, indigo and cochineal
natural dyes, found stone, glass seed
beads, waxed linen; wet felted natural
wools and silk, dyed, hand stitched
PHOTO BY JOHN LUCAS

JULIE WHITMORE

Necklace - Floral Vine,
2006
9 x 6½ x 1 inches
(22.5 x 16.3 x 2.5 cm)
Wool, beads; wet felted
PHOTO BY FRANCO PREZIO

KRISTIN LORA

Felt Ball Bracelet, 2006
1 x 7½ x ¾ inches (2.5 x 18.8 x 1.9 cm)
Silver squares, felt balls; hand fabricated,
handmade
PHOTO BY SARA STATHAS

HELENA MARETTE

Felt & Copper, 2006
10 x 1½ inches (25 x 3.8 cm)
Wool, dye, copper; wet felted, needle felted
PHOTO BY ART CASADO

NAOMI SEAGER

Untitled, 2006
5⅛ x 2¾ x 2 inches (13 x 7 x 5 cm)
Felt wool, oxidized precious metal, stainless steel wire; hand
felted, hand stitched
PHOTO BY ARTIST

BARBARA G. KILE

Coils, 2003
11 x 8 x 1 inches (27.5 x 20 x 2.5 cm)
Wool, sterling silver; wet felting, roller printing,
metal forming
PHOTO BY JACK ZILKER

Gallery

NAOMI SEAGER

Untitled, 2006
6¾ x 15¼ x 15¾ (17 x 39 x 40 cm)
Felt wool, sponge, dye, pins, thread; wet
felted, hand stitched
PHOTO BY JOHN K. MCGREGOR ECA.

JULIE WHITMORE

Necklace - Fiesta, 2006
8 x 8 x 1 inches
(20 x 20 x 2.5 cm)
Wool; wet felted, dry felted
PHOTO BY FRANCO PREZIO

GAIL CROSMAN MOORE

Magnolia, 2003
3 x 38 inches (7.5 x 96.5 cm)
Wet felted, handmade borosilicate bead,
sewn embellishments
PHOTO BY CHARLEY FRIEBERG

MIRIAM VERBEEK

Chain, 2004
13¾ x 13¾ x 1½ inches (34.9 x 34.9 x 3.8 cm)
Wool; wet felted
PHOTO BY ARTIST

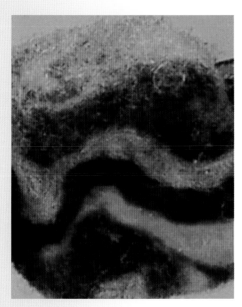

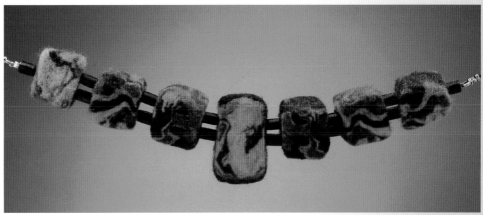

LORI FLOOD

Geode Choker, 2006
1½ x 18 x ¾ inches (3.8 x 45.7 x 1.9 cm)
Dyed wool, leather, wood beads; wet felted, sliced, hardened, strung
PHOTO BY TOM MCCOLLEY

Felted Jewelry Projects

Dramatic, playful, contemporary.

Make some, give some, wear some.

Purple Passion Set

Seed beads and bicone spacers sparkle subtly against rich purple and black spheres. Felt balls are embellished with novelty fibers and beads, then fashioned into a bracelet and matching earrings.

Bracelet

What You Need

5 grams purple wool

4 grams black wool

Black and silver novelty yarn

Black seed beads

Purple seed beads

49-strand flexible beading wire

2 crimp beads, #2

12mm toggle clasp

Crimping pliers

10 bicone spacer beads, 6mm

Upholstery or tapestry needle

Flat-nose pliers

Wire cutters

Make It

ROLL AND EMBELLISH FELT BALLS

1 Split the wool into slivers weighing one gram each, and roll into felt balls.

2 Decorate the surface of the felt beads in any fashion you like—there are so many options to try! To make this particular bracelet, you'll use seed beads, wool, and novelty fibers. First lay out the bead order. Then make a quick sketch of each bead indicating which materials you plan to use for embellishment. Remember that certain embellishments require different needs during the felting stages. For example, if you plan to needle felt a

design onto a bead, you'll need to stop felting it when the ball is still soft so you can easily add your design. Once you've completed your needle-felted design, you can finish felting.

STRING THE BALLS AND BEADS

3 String one crimp bead onto the beading wire followed by one end of the clasp. Thread the tail end of the beading wire back down through the crimp bead so that ¼ inch is on the opposite side of the crimp bead, then crimp. String one small spacer bead.

4 Make a kink in the beading wire approximately 1 inch from the opposite end, for the upholstery needle to sit.

5 Find the center of one of the felt beads and carefully twist the felt ball onto the needle. Pull the needle and wire through the bead. Repeat for the remaining felt balls. If you have trouble, use flat-nose pliers to grasp the needle and gently pull the wire through.

6 String the opposite side of the clasp and one crimp bead onto the beading wire. Thread the tail of the wire back down through the crimp bead, and pull out all the slack in the bracelet. Crimp, and trim away the excess wire.

Purple Dangle Earrings

What You Need

2 purple felt balls, .7 gram each

Purple thread

Black seed beads

Round-nose pliers

2 head pins

Flat-nose pliers

Pair of French ear wires

Make It

ROLL FELT BALLS, EMBELLISH, AND FINISH

1 Roll three purple felt balls and pick the two that match the best.

2 Stitch the black seed beads onto the felt balls in your desired pattern. Carefully twist the felt ball onto the head pin, and finish the end with a loop, using round-nose pliers. Open the loop on the French ear wire with flat-nose pliers, and hang the felt ball dangle. Finish by closing the loop.

Black Post Earrings

What You Need

2 black felt balls, .3 gram each

Black thread

Purple seed beads

Pair of earring post backs with 6mm domed cup

Multipurpose adhesive

Make It

ROLL FELT BALLS

1 I recommend rolling three black felt balls and then selecting the two that most closely match.

EMBELLISH WITH SEED BEADS

2 Anchor the black thread in the back of a black felt ball in the place where you intend to glue the post finding. Leave a small tail on the thread so you can easily find it later on. Stitch the purple seed beads in place, leaving a small bare space around the anchor stitches, since that's where you'll be gluing the earring pad. Once glued in place, the pad will cover the anchor stitches.

3 When you're done stitching the beads onto the ball, anchor your thread at the back of the bead and cut the tails.

To make a pair of earrings that match, perform each step on both felt balls before proceeding to the next step.

ATTACH THE EARRING POSTS

4 Use a toothpick to apply a layer of glue to the ear post pad. You want to apply enough glue so that it reaches the felt ball, but not so much that it oozes out the sides. Place the pad directly over the anchor stitches and hold in place a few minutes. If you think you need more glue, simply remove the post, add more glue, and try again.

Stacked Stickpins

Stack 'em up! Faceted beads provide textural interest while separating bright felted spheres, cylinders, and fanciful shapes. Wear one or multiples—the contemporary, geometric shapes make these pins ideal for mixing and matching.

What You Need

Variety of wool beads in various shapes, sizes, and colors

Seed beads, sequins, and threads for embellishing

Variety of beads

Hatpin or stickpin findings

Multipurpose adhesive

Make It

CREATE AND EMBELLISH THE FELT BEADS

1 Use a variety of wool colors to make various cube, cylinder, ball, and other shaped beads.

2 Embellish the felt beads however you wish. Add beads, threads, or leave them alone. See the Techniques section for some surface embellishing ideas.

3 I love to search for unique beads to mix with felt beads. Select both chunky and simple beads to accompany your felt beads. Lampwork and chunky, faceted glass beads can make for a playful party look, while carved wood and hand-sculpted clay beads lend a more natural and organic feel.

STACK 'EM UP

4 Support the pointed end of a stickpin between your thumb and forefinger, and, with the other hand, carefully slide the felt beads onto the stickpin. The nice thing about these pins is you can try out a stacked combination before gluing it to see if you like it or not. If you don't, simply slide all the pieces off the pin and try again.

5 Once you're satisfied with the look of the pin, replace the cap on the pointed end and slide all the pieces to the bottom next to the cap. Add a small amount of glue to the top of the stickpin, and slide the first piece into place. Repeat for each of the remaining beads, and then set the pin upside down on its "head" to dry.

Mardi Gras Bangle

B Brightly decorated with layers of felt shapes topped with seed beads, this fanciful bangle bracelet is bursting with Mardi Gras spirit. Try your hand at this one after you have a few felting projects under your belt. As you can see, the results are well worth the effort.

What You Need

1 ounce blue Merino wool roving

Plastic bangle bracelet

Small scraps of felt sheets in several colors (either handmade or commercial felt)

Multicolored seed beads

Fabric adhesive

Embroidery and sewing threads

Make It

WET FELT THE BANGLE

1 Depending on its size, more or less wool may be needed to cover your bangle bracelet. Choose a bracelet that's free of decorations and lacquers, and has an unpainted surface.

2 Tear off 8 inches of blue roving. Split the roving in half lengthwise and then split it again, creating a ¼ sliver of wool.

3 Dip the sliver into warm, soapy water and begin winding it around the bangle bracelet. Do not twist the sliver as you're winding, or the wool will not felt together smoothly. Try to wrap and overlap the wool so that you have two to three even layers of wool covering the bracelet. If you need an additional sliver to continue covering, be sure to wrap it in the same direction as the first. It takes a bit of practice to achieve a covering of wool that's consistent, so don't worry if your first attempt isn't perfect.

4 Add a bit of soap to your palms and fingers and VERY gently walk them around the bracelet, pressing gently on the fibers and taking care not to disturb the wrapped wool. Continue working in this fashion around the inside and the outside of the bracelet for several minutes. Be on the lookout for any areas where the bracelet may be showing through. If this happens, just slide the fiber back into place, or add a little wrap of fiber and work into place. Keep your hands smooth and soapy and the bracelet wet while you press on the fibers. Patience is the key during this stage of felting.

5 Once the fibers are locked together, you can begin to press and rub the bracelet with a little more pressure. Make sure to keep the piece wet, and take care to work both the inside and outside of the piece. You can also dip a piece of bubble wrap in soapy water and rub the bracelet on that. You will notice the felt beginning to tighten around the bracelet; keep increasing the pressure and agitation as this happens. Continue felting until the felt is snug around the bracelet and fully felted. Rinse thoroughly in cool water and leave to dry.

ADD EMBELLISHMENTS

6 Cut small, freeform shapes out of different colored wool sheets; I used circles, diamonds, rectangles, squares, and seed shapes. Plan out your bracelet design using the shapes. Concentric shapes can be stitched together with a straight stitch first before attaching them to the bracelet. For example, stitch the small circle on top of the big circle first, add the seed bead, and connect this to the bracelet.

Let me share a secret with you on how I ease stitching onto an awkward surface: glue the shapes in place first. This avoids having them move around. Place a few dots of glue on the back of each shape and then adhere them to the bracelet. Leave them to dry while you pick out your thread colors.

7 Anchor your thread in an inconspicuous place and use a straight stitch around each shape to add extra enforcement. Anchor the thread as you did when you started, and trim the end. Continue gluing and stitching the remaining shapes to the surface of the bracelet.

Note: Alternate fabrics, 3-D felt pieces, and embroidery stitches can also be used to embellish the bracelet's surface.

Autumnal Butterfly Pin

Make this graceful butterfly by needle felting onto a felt shape and then wet felting. The areas on the wings offer room for embellishment, allowing you to get creative with felted shapes, beads, and embroidery.

What You Need

Tracing paper

Sheet of brown acrylic/polyester
  craft felt

Foam upholstery block

10 grams brown needle felting wool

Green wool felt sheet

Turquoise wool felt sheet

Variegated cotton thread
  (in brown, green, and blue)

Pearl cotton thread
  (in turquoise and orange)

Sewing thread
  (in brown and turquoise)

Green and turquoise seed beads

.4 gram brown wool

.4 gram turquoise wool

1¼-inch pin back

Brown crayon

Make It

NEEDLE FELT THE SHAPE

1 Trace the butterfly pattern (page 109) onto tracing
  paper, and cut out. Pin the tracing paper pattern onto
the acrylic/polyester felt, and cut out the shape.

2 Set the craft felt butterfly shape onto the foam upholstery block. Needle felt brown wool into the front and
back of the butterfly shape, continuing until you have a thin
layer of wool, and can no longer see any of the brown base.

Add a bit more wool to both of the wings, but avoid needle
felting too much wool to the center where the body will be
stitched on. Once you're finished, the wool thickness on the
wings should be ½-inch thick.

WET FELT AND SHAPE

3 Saturate the butterfly in warm water. This will be a bit
  scary because you will feel that all of your hard work
sculpting has just gone out the window! But have no fear.
Add a dot of soap to your palm and rub your hands together,
dispersing the soap. Place the butterfly in between your
palms and gently smooth soap over the piece as you are agitating, or as you work the piece on soapy bubble-wrap. At
this point you are smoothing out the fibers and eliminating
the holes on the surface. Use your finger to work the "ins and
outs" of the piece, like rounding the edges
or adding definition where the big wing
meets the little wing.

4 Rinse the soap from the butterfly, and towel dry. Re-form
the piece while it's still wet. By this
I mean pinch the tips of the wings
so they come to a slight point. To
give your butterfly a more realistic
shape, fold it in half, making a crease, and
leave it to dry.

5 Make one green and one turquoise sheet of felt. They should be three to four layers of roving thick, and have a finished size of approximately 5 square inches.

EMBELLISHMENT TIME

6 Trace the large and small inner wing shape patterns onto the tracing paper. Check the patterns against your butterfly, and make any needed adjustments NOW before cutting into your precious sheets of felt. The key to the green shapes is to leave enough room between the butterfly's edge and the green piece to allow for thread embellishments. Once you're satisfied with your shapes, pin each pattern onto the green felt and cut around it. We'll call this the "right side" set. Unpin the tracing paper patterns and flip them over, repinning them to the green felt piece. Cut out the second set of shapes, or the "left side" set.

7 Position the right set onto the appropriate wings, and pin in place. Thread the needle with brown thread, and make a few anchor stitches on the back side of the butterfly, near where you want to begin stitching. Bring the needle up through the wool to the front, just inside the green wing piece. Outline each green piece using a decorative whipstitch (figure 1). Remember not to pull too tightly on your needle and thread, or all of your embroidery work will disappear.

8 Repeat the previous steps to make the turquoise inner wing shapes. Attach them using the turquoise thread and by making tiny invisible stitches (bring the needle up through the front, and then back down in nearly the same spot).

9 Thread the variegated cotton thread through a needle, double it, and make an overhand knot at the end. Bring the needle up from the back center of the butterfly, and make a running stitch outline on the large top wings in between the attached green pieces and the edge of the butterfly. Be sure to make your stitches big enough so they can be seen, and leave a gap between

stitches to allow for the orange French knots. Anchor your thread and repeat for the second side.

10 Repeat the last step, except this time using the turquoise pearl cotton thread. You don't need to worry about doubling over the thread. Make the running stitch outline around the bottom wings.

11 Using the photo as a guide, add orange French knots to the upper wings. Divide the pearl cotton strands and add running stitches or small French knots to the bottom half of the butterfly.

12 Sew green seed beads onto the turquoise areas of the upper wings, and blue seed beads to the lower wing areas.

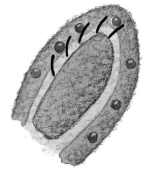

Figure 1

FELT THE BODY

13 To make your butterfly's body, weigh out .4 grams of brown and .4 grams of turquoise wool, and blend them together. Use that blended wool to wet felt an oval bead shape for the body. Depending on your butterfly, the amount of wool for the body may be a little more or less.

14 Once the body has dried, stitch it to the center of the butterfly using tiny hidden stitches. Turn the butterfly over, and attach your pin back with brown thread.

ATTACHING THE ANTENNA

15 Cut a 6-inch length of pearl cotton and make a knot in one end. Place one end of it on top of the crayon, then place a finger over the thread. Pull the other end of the thread so that it makes a light coating of brown wax over the thread. Repeat to achieve the desired effect. Thread the now-waxed pearl cotton through a needle, and thread it through the top of the body. Remove the needle, making another knot at the end of the thread. Trim the ends of the cotton.

Couture Necklace

Cloisonné baubles crown bead-encrusted felt balls to make multiple dangling

pendants. Since you custom-cut a chain to your own desired length, it's easy

to add or subtract felt and pearl pendants to suit your taste.

What You Need

2.5 grams of turquoise wool

Turquoise seed beads

12 gold head pins, 2 inches long

12 gold bead caps, 8mm

6 faux pearls, 15mm

6 faux pearls, 6mm

Wire cutters

Round-nose pliers

12 round gold beads, 4mm

6 cloisonné beads, 8mm

18 inches of gold chain, 9.4mm

Flat-nose pliers

10mm gold hook and eye clasp

5mm gold jump ring

Make It

STRING FELT BALLS AND BEADS

1 Split the wool into .5-gram slivers, and roll five felt balls. Stitch the seed beads in a random pattern onto the felt balls and set aside.

2 String a gold bead cap, a large pearl, another gold bead cap, and then a small pearl onto a gold head pin. Finish the end of the head pin by making a loop and trimming away the excess wire. Repeat this five more times for a total of six pearl-beaded head pins.

3 Thread a gold bead, a felt ball, a cloisonné bead, and then another gold bead onto a head pin. Finish the end with a loop, taking care not to put tension on the beads, as that will result in felt beads that look squashed versus round. Repeat this four more times for a total of five felt-beaded head pins.

ATTACH THE FINDINGS

4 A princess length necklace measures from 17 to 19 inches. You can purchase a chain that's ready-to-wear, or order minimum quantities of unfinished chain from a jewelry supply company. If you choose the latter, cut the chain to the desired length. To attach the clasp, use flat-nose pliers to open the loop on the hook, and connect it to the end of the chain. Be sure to close the loop securely so that there are no gaps for it to come unattached. Connect the other side of the clasp with the gold jump ring. Use flat-nose pliers to open the ring from side to side, and then attach the chain to the loop with the jump ring. Close the ring snugly.

5 For a special touch, I like to add a beaded embellishment to the clasp end of my pieces. String a gold bead, a cloisonné bead, and then another gold bead onto a head pin and finish the end with a loop. Open the loop and hang the beaded dangle from the loop end of the clasp. Finish by closing the loop.

6 Open the loops on all of the felt and pearl dangles. Find the bottom center link of the chain, hang the first felt dangle, and close the loop. Now skip one link of chain to both the right and left of the felt dangle and hang a pearl dangle on each side. Repeat this sequence, alternating felt and pearl dangles. Work your way up both sides of the necklace until you have attached all the beaded dangles.

Luscious Fruit Earrings

Dangly, felted cherry and berry earrings show off your playful side. Suspended on delicate wires, these petite fruits can be adorned with your choice of either beads or embroidered French knots.

Cherry Earrings

What You Need

2 grams red Merino wool

Red seed beads

Red thread

20-gauge brown craft wire

Round-nose pliers

2 side drilled leaf beads, 7 x 11mm

Multipurpose adhesive

Pair of brown niobium ear wires

Make It

ROLL FELT BALLS

I work the steps to make both earrings simultaneously, felting a little on one, and then switching to the other. This helps to keep the pair looking similar in size and shape. The same goes for embellishing.

1 Divide the wool into .2 to .3 gram pieces and roll three balls. Pick out the two that best match each other.

2 Anchor your thread on one of the felt balls and stitch the red seed beads on in a random pattern.

MAKE AND ATTACH THE EAR WIRES

3 Cut two 1½-inch lengths of brown wire. Make a loop at one end of each of the wires using round-nose pliers, and then slide on a leaf bead. Carefully twist the felt cherry bead onto the wire. Make a very small hook at the bottom of the wire to keep the cherry in place and prevent it from falling off the wire (figure 1).

Figure 1

4 Place a small amount of glue just above the hook, and slide and twist the cherry down over it. Now put a small amount of glue just below the top loop and slide the leaf bead up next to the loop. Be sure that as you leave the piece to dry, the loop next to the leaf bead is parallel to the leaf bead.

5 Once the pieces have dried, you can make a slight curve in the wire by placing the curved part of your thumb on the middle of the wire between the leaf and cherry, and adding a slight amount of pressure to either end. Easy does it here!

6 Open the loops on the ear wires and connect the cherry dangles. Finish by closing the loops.

What You Need

.4 grams pink Merino wool

Light pink embroidery floss

Multipurpose adhesive

2 silver eye pins

2 silver leaf bead caps, 8.7mm

Pair of silver ear wires

Make It

ROLL FELT BALLS

1 Split the wool in half so that each berry will weigh .2 grams. Roll the sliver up like when you make a felt ball, and felt. Since this is such a small amount of wool, it can be easily manipulated in the final stages of felting. Once you're nearly finished felting, take the tip of your index finger and apply pressure to one end of

the felt ball, rubbing it back and forth on your work mat, creating a tapered end. When the pair is complete, rinse, reshape, and leave to dry.

ADD FRENCH KNOTS

2 From here on, I'll refer to the two ends of the berry shape as the "round end" (where the bead cap will sit), and the "pointed end" (tapered tip). Split the embroidery floss into single strands. Anchor the thread on the round end of the berry shape, and then poke the needle straight down through the center core, exiting at the pointed tip. Begin by making one French knot at the tip, and then continue covering the remaining surface of the berry in a random pattern. Take care not to make any French knots where your bead cap will be placed, or it won't sit level. When you're finished making French knots, anchor the thread where you started, and trim.

ATTACH EYE PINS

3 Sand the wire on the eye pins. Trim the eye pins at an angle so there's ½ inch of wire below the loop.

4 Add a drop of glue to the inside of the bead cap and position it on top of the berry.

5 Add a little bit of glue to the eye pin wire and twist the pointed end through the hole in the bead cap, down into the felt berry (figure 1). Locate your "favorite" side of each earring, and position the loop on the eye pin so that the best sides will face front. Turn the loop to whichever way you want to be the "front," and set aside to dry.

Figure 1

6 After the pieces have dried, open the loop on each ear wire and hang the berry shapes. Finish by closing the loops.

Priestess Collar Necklace

Like the limelight? Then this necklace is for you. The attention-grabbing

collar encircles your neck with variegated and graduating felt coils, and

features a clever felted self-closure.

What You Need

2 ounces charcoal Merino wool

2 ounces light gray Merino wool

Felting Needle

Upholstery or tapestry needle

Flexible beading wire

2 crimp beads, #2

Make It

CREATE FELTED COILS

1 Start by making the center coil and work your way outward, two coils at a time—this will help keep the thicknesses and sizes consistent. I recommend lining the knotted coils up next to each other in the order that they will be strung. That way you can see if you need to remake a coil or untie a coil and felt it some more. Don't worry if your coils are not perfectly graduated. If you stick close to the plan of subtracting the length and a little thickness (see the Coil Measurements chart), the effect will still be present.

2 Decide how thick and long you want your center coil, keeping in mind that the felt coil will shrink approximately one-third in size. The twist test mentioned in the Techniques section will help you to determine the coils' felted thicknesses. There are forty-seven coils on this necklace. I suggest wearing rubber gloves when making the coils because there are so many and it helps speed agitation. The Coil Measurement chart gives the thicknesses and lengths of the coil measurements

BEFORE they are felted. The thickness is gauged from using normal Merino roving. For example, ¼ means I divide the roving in half and then those two sides were halved again. It gets a little tricky to keep the roving at consistent thicknesses once you get down to the ⅛-inch slivers. Most of the slivers toward the end are approximately ¼ to ⅛-inch in length. Instead of trying to make precise measurements with short lengths and skinny slivers, I make adjustments with scissors and then re-felt.

3 After a coil is felted completely, tie a single knot in the middle of it. Hold the knot between two fingers and, with the other hand, pull the tails downward from the knot. Place the knotted coil on the work mat and roll it back and forth, keeping the tails together as you roll. Rinse out the soap using cool water. Scrunch the tails to make them crinkle, and leave to dry.

BUTTON CLASP

4 To create the button part of the clasp, make an extra ¼ x by 9-inch coil and tie it in a knot as you did with the others. It's best if you can make a coil that is ¼ inch thick in the middle and tapers toward the ends. This will minimize bulk later on.

5 For the loop end of the clasp, felt another ¼ x by 9-inch sliver that measures 1 inch in the middle,

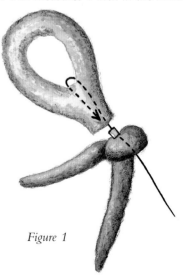

Figure 1

keeping the sides as dry as possible so they don't felt. Set the 1-inch portion on top of your index finger, and wrap the two unfelted ends down around your finger. Keep the ring around your finger, and felt the two ends together like a normal coil. Once the two ends are connected, you can work the loop part of the coil, but check the size often against the button knot. If the loop gets too small, use scissors to snip open the inside of the loop near the bottom where the two ends came together. Rinse and leave the loop to dry. Once the button end of the clasp is dry, wrap a small sliver of roving tightly around the two ends. The goal is to mask the two tails, making them look like one. If the two ends are too thick when they are put together, use scissors to trim a little of the inside thickness of the coil away. Once you have an overall round shape, wrap it with roving, and needle felt. Re-wet and soap the coil-end of the button, and felt it as if you were making a coil. Rinse away the soap and let it dry.

PUT IT ALL TOGETHER

6 Use a large needle to string the coils onto the beading wire. Poke the needle through the side of a knot. Note the orientation of the tails when strung; they should lie like a pair of open scissors, not on their sides like a "V". As you string, check to make sure the knots align next to each other.

7 Trim the clasp ends so they are even in length. String one crimp bead onto the wire and rethread the needle with wire. Put the needle through the loop end of the clasp so it comes out at the inside bottom of the loop. Put the needle back down through just next to where it came up (as shown in figure 1). Remove the needle and put the tail through the crimp bead and crimp. Slide all the knots to the side of the secured clasp. The button side of the clasp can be connected

Coil Measurements

Number one is the center coil so you need only make one of those. Number two and onward should all be made in pairs.

Coil position number	thickness of roving or sliver	length of sliver
Center	½"	16"
2	½"	16"
3	½"	16"
4	⅓"	14"
5	⅓"	14"
6	⅓"	14"
7	¼"	12"
8	¼"	12"
9	¼"	10"
10	¼"	10"
11	¼"	10"
12	¼"	10"
13	¼"	9"
14	¼"	9"
15	¼"	9"
16	⅛"	8"
17	⅛"	8"
18	⅛"	8"
19	⅛"	7"
20	⅛"	7"
21	⅛"	6"
22	⅛"	6"
23	⅛"	5¼"
24	⅛"	5¼"

Are your coils too long? Remember, you can snip the ends at an angle, add some soap and water, and re-felt by rolling the tips back and forth on the work mat.

just like the loop end, except bring the needle through the center of the knot and back down through. Remove all the excess wire, and crimp.

An easier, but just as sophisticated, variation of this necklace is to make all the coils the same length and size, and string them.

Flying Heart Brooch

One look at this winged brooch will make you feel lighthearted. Tiny multicolored beads are sprinkled across a vivid red heart that has sprouted periwinkle wings. The wings are stiffened and then enlivened with colored pencils.

What You Need

Tracing paper

Sharp scissors

Sheet of red acrylic/polyester craft felt

Foam work surface

3 grams red wool (for needle felting)

Felting needle

Blue Merino felt sheet

Fabric stiffener

Colored pencils

Multi-colored seed beads

1-inch pin back

Sewing thread

Multipurpose adhesive

Make It

NEEDLE FELT THE HEART

1 Trace the heart shape pattern (see page 110) onto tracing paper, and cut out. Pin the tracing paper pattern onto the acrylic/polyester craft felt and use sharp scissors to cut out the shape.

2 Set the shape onto your foam work surface. Tear off a small tuft of wool and begin needle felting it into the red craft felt heart. Continue felting until you have an even layer of wool covering the heart. Remember, you can poke the wool from any direction to make an area tighter or to draw it in. I often have to do a little extra forming with the needle in the area where the heart comes to a "V," and at the bottom tip of the heart to make it taper. Turn the heart over and needle felt a thin layer of wool on the back side.

Flip the piece back over so that the front is showing, and continue building up thickness. Keep adding wool until the piece is ⅜ inch thick. Wet felt the heart for a few minutes until it is smooth and the fibers are tight. Rinse the heart, reshape it, and set the piece aside while it dries.

CREATE AND EMBELLISH THE WINGS

3 Trace and cut out the wing pattern. Pin the pattern onto the blue sheet of felt, and cut it out. To stiffen the wings, dip them in fabric stiffener and lay them out to dry.

4 Once dry, I used blue, light blue, purple, lavender, and white colored pencils to embellish the stiffened felt wings. Use small, light, circular motions with the pencil to add color.

5 Stitch the multicolored beads onto the heart in a random pattern. Turn the piece over and position the pin back and wings to make sure there is enough space for gluing and stitching. The ends of the wings should meet together or have a little space between them, but not overlap. Make any adjustments to the wings by trimming. When you're satisfied, use needle and thread to stitch on the pin back. Add a little glue to the front side of the wings where the heart will sit, and glue them to the back of the heart.

Vintage Lace Choker

U

Use one of your grandma's doilies, or a lacy flea market find to make this enchanting choker. During the felting process, the piece of lace becomes entangled with the wool's fibers; holding it snugly in place.

What You Need

4 grams burgundy Merino wool

Small lace doily, 2½ inches in diameter

Sponge

Bubble wrap

Cordless sander with felting
  attachment (optional)

Black satin ribbon

Fabric sealer (to prevent fraying)

Thread (black and burgundy)

Black iridescent seed beads

Ribbon clamp ends (size depends on
  ribbon width)

Hook for clasp

2 jump rings, 5mm

1 to 2 inches of silver chain

Iridescent black 8mm faceted bead

4 black 6mm faceted beads

Silver head pin

Flat-nose pliers

Make It

WET FELT THE DOILY WITH THE WOOL

1 Lay four layers of wool out on your work mat so that there's one additional inch of wool framing the doily. Place the doily on top of the layers of wool.

2 Place your hand on top of the wool pile and use a sponge to gently wet the layers, being careful not to disturb the wool pile. Add a drop of soap, a layer of bubble wrap, and while taking all the necessary safety precautions, use a sander to felt the piece. Once the layers are holding together, remove the bubble wrap and continue felting, turning the piece frequently to work both sides. If parts of the doily get felted together, tug out sections of the wool, reopening holes in the doily.

EMBELLISH AND ATTACH THE RIBBON

5 Measure the diameter of your neck where you want the ribbon to sit. Cut the ribbon to that length, and add a line of fabric sealer to each of the edges to prevent raveling.

6 Anchor the black thread about ½ inch in from the edge of the ribbon, and then stitch on iridescent black seed beads every ¼ inch. When you come to the opposite end, leave a 1½-inch gap. Repeat on the other ribbon edge.

7 Fold the end edge of the ribbon under ¼ inch and finish it with the clamp end finding. Repeat for the opposite side. Open a 5mm jump ring, and connect the piece of chain to the clamp end finding. Use the other jump ring to connect the hook end of the clasp. String the 8mm bead, followed by a 6mm black bead, onto a head pin and finish with a loop. Connect this embellishment piece to the end of the chain.

ASSEMBLE THE PIECES

8 Anchor the burgundy thread to the back side of the felted lace piece, and stitch three black beads to the center. Highlight the doily's pattern by selectively stitching iridescent seed beads onto the surface.

9 Decide where you want the flower to sit on the ribbon (off to either side or in the middle), and position the flower so that it's not too top heavy, causing it to flop forward when being worn. You can check this by pinning it in place and trying it on. Finish by stitching the flower securely to the ribbon.

FORM A FLOWER

3 Make a flower out of the felted piece following the Making a Flower from a Flat Sheet of Felt steps in the Techniques section.

4 Once the piece is fully felted, rinse it in cool water, pull out any closed holes in the doily, and towel dry. Use scissors to trim away the unfinished edge, leaving a small border and following the doily edge as a guide. Reshape and leave to dry.

Sassy Party Rings

Slip on one (or more) of these flashy little rings, and let the party begin! Almost as much fun to make as to wear, these little jewels are embellished with embroidered metallic asterisks, loops of seed beads, and dangly sparkles.

Pink Ring

What You Need

.5 gram pink felt ball

Silver seed beads

Upholstery or tapestry needle

Clear beading elastic

13 to 14 assorted 6mm faceted beads

Crimp bead

Crimping tool

Make It

ROLL AND EMBELLISH A FELT BALL

1 Roll a pink felt ball. Anchor the thread, and stitch seed beads in clusters of three onto the felt ball.

CREATE THE RING BAND

2 Thread a large-eyed needle with clear beading elastic, and string the bottom portion of the felt ball on the needle and cord (see figure 1). Trim the cord, leaving three inches on either side of the felt ball.

3 String 6mm faceted beads onto each end of the elastic tails. Once you have reached the desired size, string one crimp bead onto the cord. Thread the other end of the cord in the opposite direction through the crimp bead, and crimp. An alternate way to finish the ends would be to tie them in a snug knot with a dot of glue to secure them, and trim.

Figure 1

Black Ring

What You Need

.3 grams black wool

Felting needle

Seed beads

6mm faceted
center focal
bead

Adjustable ring shank
with a gluing pad

Multipurpose adhesive

Make It

CREATE AND EMBELLISH THE FELT BEAD

1 Roll a sliver of black wool into a coil, and needle felt the sides. If needed, you can add a little bit of wool to the top or bottom to add some thickness. Wet felt the shape to smooth and round the edges.

2 Anchor the thread on the back side of the felt disc, and stitch the focal bead to the center. Add seed beads around the focal bead and on the disc's sides. Anchor the thread on the backside, and trim.

ATTACH THE BEAD

3 Place a dot of glue on the pad of the ring, and set the felt piece in place. Gently hold the ring and felt piece in place for a few minutes while the glue sets up.

Purple Ring

What You Need

.5 gram purple felt ball

Silver metallic embroidery floss

Ring-sized memory wire

Round-nose pliers

Black seed beads

8 faceted beads in desired
colors, 4mm

8 silver head pins, 1 inch long

Make It

ROLL AND EMBELLISH A FELT BALL

1 Roll a purple felt ball. Use silver metallic embroidery floss to stitch a silver asterisk or star pattern onto the felt ball.

MAKE THE RING BAND

2 Cut off one piece of ring-sized memory wire so that it is two full coil lengths. Use round-nose pliers to finish one end of the memory wire with a small loop. Position the loop so that it is sitting upward from the rest of the coil.

3 String the black seed beads onto the memory wire until they almost fill the loop, leaving an approximate ¼-inch gap for the felt ball. Slide the lower portion of the felt ball onto the memory wire and up against the last seed bead (see figure 1). Continue stringing seed beads. As you approach the end of the wire, leave enough space to make another loop to match the first.

4 String one 4mm faceted bead onto each of the head pins, and finish the end of the wire with a loop. Open a loop on the beaded dangle and connect it to one of the loops on the ring. Repeat so that there are a total of four bead dangles on each of the ring's two loops.

Funky Hair Bands

How about a little jewelry for your hair? You can make one of these spiky bands lickety-split to go with your favorite outfit. Little and big girls alike will appreciate the "cool" factor of these coil hair bands, so they make great gifts.

What You Need

4 to 5 grams Merino wool

Thick black rubber hair band

5 felt coils measuring:

  One 12-inch length

  Two 10-inch lengths

  Two 7½-inch lengths

Make It

MAKE FELT COILS

1 Divide the wool into slivers. Felt the longest middle coil first, and then work your way down in size. Use the measurements above, or make the coils to suit your personality: long, short, spaghetti thin. There's no right or wrong way to make these—they always end up looking great! To make a rainbow coil, lay tiny multicolored wool slivers in a row on top of the work surface, then lay a base sliver of wool (in this case black) on top of the colored slivers.

2 Tear off more multicolored slivers and place them on top of the base sliver. Felt the slivers as you would a coil and the other colors will work their way in as you roll.

ATTACH THE COILS

3 Fold the 12-inch coil in half so that the two ends meet up. Put the looped end of the coil through the middle of the hair band. Bring the ends of the coil up and over the hair band and through the coil's loop, pulling them snug. Slide this coil over the seam on the hair band to hide it.

4 Add the next two coils to the right and left of the 12-inch coil. Repeat for the last two coils.

5 Slide the coils against each other and position them so that the tails point outward from the center of the circle, like sunrays.

Tasseled Seaside Lariat

As if caught in a sea breeze, delicate chain tassels sway gracefully beneath transparent beads and embellished felt balls. Silver head pins are threaded with colored and faceted beads, and then artfully grouped on the lariat chain.

What You Need

2 green felt balls, .5 gram each

Turquoise seed beads

2 silver eye pins, 2 inches long

2 round silver beads, 3mm

7 faceted champagne-colored beads, 8mm

Round-nose pliers

2 silver tassels, 40mm in length

5 silver head pins, 2 inches long

5 turquoise Austrian crystal beads, 5mm

Approximately 2-meter length of silver chain, 3mm

Wire cutters

Make It

ROLL AND EMBELLISH THE FELT BALLS

1 Roll two green .5 gram felt balls. Anchor your thread on the felt bead, and stitch on turquoise seed beads. When finished, anchor and then trim your thread. Repeat for the second bead.

TASSEL AND DANGLE PIECES

2 String one silver bead on the eye pin, followed by a felt bead, then a faceted bead, and then finishing the end with a loop. Open the loop next to the silver bead, connect the tassel, and close the loop, completing the first bead tassel piece. Repeat this step to complete the pair.

3 String one faceted bead onto a head pin followed by a 5mm turquoise bead, and finish the end with a loop. Repeat this four more times for a total of five beaded dangles.

ASSEMBLE IT

4 Wrap the chain around your neck so that the two tails are hanging down the front. Decide on the desired length, and make adjustments by trimming the end of the chain.

5 Open the loop on the end of the tassel piece and connect it to one end of the chain. Close the loop. Repeat for the other tassel.

6 Open the loops on the other beaded dangles. Wrap the chain around your neck in the fashion that you plan on wearing the finished piece. Connect the beaded dangles so that they are interspersed along the chain. I placed three so that they hang near my neck, and the other two on the part of the chain that hangs down the front.

NOTE: Matching earrings can be created by making matching felt ball beads or with a pair of extra bead dangles.

Mixed Media Brooches

These brooches are ideal for showcasing tiny works of art. Diminutive, scalloped-edged felt frames hold and highlight everything from a favorite photo or scrap of vintage lace, to a colorful bottle cap. They can be embellished with contrasting felt, decorative stitching, and beads.

What You Need

Merino wool in various colors
(approx. 5 grams per object)

Found object

Bubble wrap

Cordless sander with felting
attachment (optional)

Small sharp scissors

Embroidery threads

Scissors or pinking shears

1-inch pin back

Make It

SELECT YOUR OBJECT

1 Choosing an object to be felted into your piece is
really fun. Having experimented with many types
of objects, I have found that what works best are
objects that are waterproof, and are no thicker than ¼
inch.

LAY OUT THE WOOL

2 The thickness and number of wool layers required
for a brooch depends on the thickness and shape
of your object. For thicker objects, a little more wool is
needed on the base layers in order to support it.

If an object is 1-inch in diameter, add a border of 4 or
so inches. For example, if your object is a bottle cap
measuring 1 ¼ inches in diameter, lay out your wool so
that it's at least 5 inches round. That way you'll have
plenty of room to trim away the rough edges, or in
case the object gets a little off-center during felting.

3 Begin by laying out three layers of your back-
ground color wool on your work surface. Lay the

fibers out as if you were making a sheet of felt. Set the object in the middle of the wool pile and add a small tuft of wool that only covers the object, not the whole wool pile. Sometimes I make this wool a different color so that when the hole is cut, you can see the wool layers. Add three more layers of wool on top of the object. For added embellishment, you can add a cobweb layer of wool to the top, or an extra ring of wool or novelty fibers around your object.

WET FELT

4 Add a drop of soap to your pile of wool, and gently drizzle on some warm, soapy water, taking care not to disturb the layers of wool. Place a small sheet of bubble wrap on top of the wool pile, and then place a sander directly on the top center of your object. This is where it gets tricky because you don't want your object to scoot around in the wool layers. In order to prevent this, keep one finger on the object, and then use the sander to work around its perimeter.

5 Once your fibers have locked into place, remove the bubble wrap and continue felting by using the sander directly on the wool. If you prefer not to use a sander, substitute your hands and bubble wrap instead. Just pat the layers of the wool with your hands

to begin the felting process. Turn the piece over frequently to ensure that both sides of the object get felted evenly. At this point, keep using your finger to hold the object in place while working the sander all the way around it, pushing the sander's edge up against the object. Again, if you choose not to use a sander, you can use the bubble side of the bubble wrap to work the edge up against the object.

6 When the object is firmly set in place and the piece is nearly fully felted, use small, sharp scissors to carefully cut a SMALL hole in the middle, creating a window. The goal is to leave enough wool on top of the object to create a bezel that will hold the object in place between the layers. I can't emphasize how important it is to take away just a little wool at a time. Bear in mind that the wool will stretch and pull a little when you're finishing, resulting in an even bigger hole. If, once you have completed the felting, you're not satisfied with the size of the hole, then you can carefully trim away a bit more wool. It's okay if your object still slides a little; you can secure it in place with a few stitches around the border.

7 Rinse the soapy water out of your brooch, and towel dry. Straighten it into your final desired shape, and leave to dry.

DECORATE THE BORDER

8 Make a mental note of how much wool you would like to leave for your border. Use threads, beads, needle felting, and embroidery to embellish the border of your object. I leave the rough border intact so I have something to hold onto while I'm stitching and embellishing. Once you're finished embellishing, carefully cut away the rough edge.

9 Turn the piece over, and adhere the pin back with a needle and thread.

Chic Rosebud Hatpin

The classical beauty of the rose is captured in this felted hatpin. The variegated petals are made by wrapping mohair-blended wool around a bottle form and then wet felting.

What You Need

8 grams pink wool*

Small plastic bottle (a sample shampoo bottle works well)

Bubble wrap

3 grams moss green wool (for needle felting)

Sheet of green acrylic/polyester craft felt

10mm pink round bead

Multipurpose adhesive

Silver stickpin finding

Moss green sewing thread

Moss green seed beads

*I used a blended wool that had mohair in it for texture.

Make It

WET FELT THE PETALS

1 Follow the instructions for felting around a form in the Techniques section. To create the form for the rose, I used a small astringent bottle. The diameter of the bottle's body was 1⅜ inches, and the neck was ⅞ inches in diameter. The rose has an inside and an outside set of petals that will be felted separately. First, felt the outside "petals" by wrapping the pink wool around the bottle's body, and then down the neck (figure 1). Wet felt. Repeat the same process to make the inside "petals," but wrap the wool around the bottle's neck plus a little of the body (figure 2).

2 You'll know it's safe to pull the petal piece off the form when you see that the fibers have locked into place and are not sliding around on the bottle. Check the inside of the petal to see if it has felted. If not, use your soapy fingers or some bubble wrap to work the inside of the petals.

Figure 1

Figure 2

REFINE THE PETALS

3 Roll the bottom end of the petal piece back and forth on your work mat, like a coil, to make it more tapered. Next make a ripple-like edge on the petal by placing your index finger on the edge of the rose and sliding it back and forth on bubble wrap. This action will pull that area of wool in a bit. Skip a little space and repeat for the remainder of the edge. You can also trim the edge with scissors for a more crisp and controlled rippled edge. Repeat for the inside rose piece.

CREATE THE LEAVES

4 Needle felt two leaves with the moss green wool proportionate to your rose's size. You can use the pattern for the leaves in the Poppy Necklace as a guide (page 110). Be careful not to needle felt the leaves too thick; they need to be flexible. Once you're finished needle felting the leaves, wet felt them.

ASSEMBLE THE PIECES

5 Place a small dot of adhesive at the top of the stickpin finding, and slide the 10mm bead all the way up next to the head. Set the piece aside while it dries. Put the pin finding down through the center of the small rose and then slide it up toward the top so that the bead shows. Mark a spot on the pin to show where the bottom edge of the inner rose sits, and place some glue at that spot. Slide the inner rose piece into place. If you have too much material bulk at the bottom of the small rose, carefully trim it away so that the outside rose piece can sit up against it. Slide the outside rose piece into place and attach it to the pin finding like you did with the inner rose.

6 Anchor your thread and stitch green seed beads onto the leaves, using the project photo as a guide for placement.

7 Poke the stickpin through the bottom edge of the left-hand leaf, and slide it up until it's flush with the rose. Pinch the two bottom sides of the leaf so that it conforms to the base of the rose. Use a straight stitch to keep the pinched edges together. Add a little glue on the pin to help secure the leaf in place, and then tack the leaf to the rose with a felting needle. Repeat for the second leaf, except pinching the two edges around the first leaf. Use a straight stitch to connect the second leaf's edges to the first leaf. You can mask the straight stitches by stitching seed beads up the front in a linear fashion.

Abstract Brooch Trio

When you unleash your imagination and combine stylized felted shapes with beads and embroidery, the results can make a fashion statement. Perfect for business attire as well as casual wear, pin one on a jacket, hat, or scarf for a contemporary touch.

What You Need

Tracing paper

Sheet of gold acrylic/polyester craft felt

4 grams gold Wilde wool

2 grams gold Merino wool

Felting needle

Sandpaper

10 small straight pins

Multipurpose glue

10 brownish-purple beads, 8mm

Gold sewing thread

1¼-inch pin back

Wire cutters

Make It

NEEDLE FELT THE RING

1 Trace the ring pattern (refer to page 109) onto tracing paper, and cut it out. Transfer the shape onto the craft felt, and cut out.

2 Cover the ring shape by needle felting a 1-inch-thick layer of gold Wilde wool onto the front, and a thin layer on the back. Wrap and needle felt a sliver or two of gold Merino wool evenly around the ring shape so that it makes the edges look more rounded. This will also help cover the back of the felt base.

WET FELT THE PIECE

3 Wet the ring shape in warm soapy water, add a drop of dish soap to your fingers, and lightly felt the surface, smoothing out any holes resulting from the needle felting. Rinse the felt piece in cool water, towel dry, and reform the ring shape. Leave the piece to dry.

FINISH UP

4 Lightly sand the straight pins so the glue has a rough surface to adhere to. Add a drop of multi-purpose glue near the head of the pin, and slide a brownish/purple bead onto the pin. Repeat for the remaining pins and beads, and then leave to dry.

5 Stitch the pin back to the back of the piece. Place some glue on the bottom lip of one of the beads and along the pin, and stick the pin into the edge of the ring shape. Don't worry if the tip of a pin sticks out in the center of the ring. Work the remaining pins into the ring, and leave the piece to dry. If some of the pins poked through to the middle of the ring, carefully trim them flush to the felt surface with wire cutters.

Turquoise Triangle Brooch

What You Need

Tracing paper

Sheet of turquoise and sheet of charcoal
 gray acrylic/polyester craft felt

6 grams turquoise Wilde wool

Felting needle

Orange wool felt sheet

Purple pearl cotton thread

1¼-inch pin back

Short straight pins

Sandpaper

Multipurpose adhesive

Turquoise seed beads

Make It

NEEDLE FELT THE TRIANGLE

1 Repeat the needle felt steps as outlined for making the Gold Brooch except use the turquoise craft
felt sheet to create a triangle base (pattern on page
109), and needle felt it with the turquoise Wilde wool.
Do not wet felt this piece.

ADD FELT PIECES AND EMBELLISH

2 Set the triangle on top of the orange sheet and
trace around it with a pen. Cut the orange triangle out so that it is slightly smaller than the turquoise
triangle.

3 Cut two 6 x ⁵⁄₁₆-inch strips from the gray felt.
Thread a needle with purple embroidery thread,
and stitch a running stitch down one side of each strip.
Tuck the front ends of the two strips down underneath
the center of the triangle and around to the backside.
Wrap the opposite ends of the strips over the top,
around to the back, and pin at the seam where the
two ends overlap. Secure the four ends by gluing or
stitching.

4 Stitch the orange triangle onto the back of the
turquoise triangle. Decide how you would like the
triangle to sit when being worn, and stitch the pin
back to the back of the triangle in that orientation.

5 Decorate the triangle with randomly placed
beaded pins. See step 5 of the Gold Brooch for
how to adhere pins.

Striped Brooch

What You Need

Tracing paper

Sheet of brown acrylic/polyester craft felt

3 to 4 grams brown Hampshire needle felting wool

Felting needle

1 gram fuchsia Hampshire needle felting wool

Blue pearl cotton thread

Green locks

Brown sewing thread

1-inch pin back

Make It

NEEDLE FELT THE TRIANGLE

1   Repeat the needle felt steps as outlined for making the Gold Brooch except use brown craft felt to create a triangle base (pattern on page 109), and needle felt it with a ¼-inch-thick layer of brown wool. Needle felt the tip and two thin, curved stripes onto the triangle using the fuchsia wool.

EMBELLISH AND FINISH UP

2   Thread your needle with the blue embroidery thread, and anchor on the back side of the triangle. Bring the needle and thread up through the felt next to the edge of a fuchsia stripe. Outline each of the fuchsia-striped edges with a running stitch. Anchor the thread on the back again, and trim the tail.

3   Green locks can be needle felted into and along the top edge of the triangle. Finish the brooch by stitching on the pin back just below the green locks.

Geometric Hair Clips

Tame that stray strand of hair with a stylish clip. A burnished button accent sits atop concentrically increasing squares, circles, and triangles. These are quick and easy to make, requiring only small sheets of felt and bobby pins.

What You Need

Tracing paper

2 sheets of wool (per barrette), each 2 x 2 inches

Flat silver bead or buttons

Needle and sewing thread

Seed beads

Bobby pins with gluing pad

Multipurpose adhesive

Make It

CUT OUT THE SHAPES

1 Trace a large and small geometric shape of your choice (see page 110) onto tracing paper, and cut out. Pin the larger shape pattern onto a sheet of felt, and the smaller pattern onto a different colored sheet. Cut them out.

ASSEMBLE THE PIECES

2 Stack the pieces together with the large wool shape on the bottom, then the small wool shape, with the silver button on top.

3 Stitch the pieces together by poking a needle with thread down through the middle of the three layers, and then back up. String one seed bead onto the thread, and tie the two ends in a snug knot. Trim, leaving a little tail on the thread ends.

4 Place a dot of glue on the bobby pin's pad and then position the felt piece in place. Set the piece aside to dry, with the silver button facedown. Rest the opposite end of the bobby pin on top of a magazine to avoid the bobby pin sliding out of place while drying.

African Sunset Cuff

Ever yearn to go on safari? With their exotic stripes and spots, these beads feature patterns that mimic those of the cheetah, giraffe, and zebra. Two rows of beading elastic are threaded through the tapered, cylindrical-shaped beads, making the cuff easy to slip on and off.

What You Need

12 oval Merino beads, 1.3 to 1.5 grams of
   wool per bead, (4 white, 8 black)*

24 black round beads, 6mm

Black beading elastic

2 grams blended fuchsia and red Merino
   wool (for embellishing)

1 gram black Merino wool (for embellishing)

* The four white beads and four of the eight
   black beads must be only partially felted to
   allow for needle-felted embellishment.
   Finished oval bead size is ½" x 2" to 2½" in
   the middle.

Make It

FELT PATTERNS ON THE BEADS

1 Set the four finished black oval beads aside.
   Needle felt simple patterns such as polka dots,
stripes, and zigzags onto the remaining felt beads. Be
sure to really work the design into the bead with the
felting needle so it will stay in place when wet felting.

2 Continue by wet felting the beads until the needle-
   felted pattern is level with the base bead. You'll
quickly notice why it's so important to thoroughly needle
felt the pattern into the oval bead. The fibers will pull a
little, dulling some of your crisp lines. If you notice that
the pattern is blurring badly, stop felting and let the
beads dry. Then you can go back and needle felt again.
Rinse the beads in cool water, and leave them to dry.

STRING IT TOGETHER

3 String one round black bead onto the beading
   elastic. Thread a large needle with beading elastic.
Find the center of one of the oval beads and then move
outward approximately ¼ inch. Put the needle through
the center (widthwise) of the bead. These measurements are merely a guide. Depending on your spacer
beads, you may want to space your two strands of elastic closer or farther apart. I found that when I spaced
my elastic strands farther apart, the elastic showed in
between the beads due to their tapered shape.

4 Continue this pattern using the remainder of the
   felt beads, resulting in one-half of the cuff being
strung. Leave a 3-inch tail of elastic, and trim.

5 Work the second half of the cuff exactly as the
   first half, except this time string the elastic
through the left side of center (see figure 1).

6 Now's the time to check the size and length of
   the cuff to your wrist. Adjustments in length can
be made by either adding or subtracting black spacer
or felt beads. Please note that it's normal for the beads
not to be perfectly aligned due to the wonderful handmade nature of the piece.

7 Tie the two corresponding ends of elastic in a
   snug knot, and trim the ends.

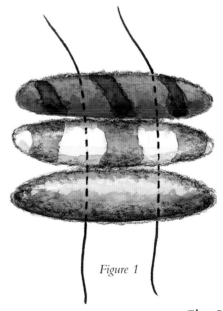

Figure 1

Wild Poppy Blooms

When a stunning accessory is called for, reach for this necklace. Reminiscent of the much-loved poppy, these red felt petals, subtly tinged with gold, surround soft brown centers. A matching ring completes the look.

Poppy Necklace

What You Need

Tracing paper

Sheet of green acrylic/polyester craft felt

1.5 ounces dark and light green blended roving

Felting needle

.7 gram green felt ball

1 ounce red Merino roving

5 grams orange roving

5 grams yellow/gold roving

Cordless sander with felting attachment (optional)

1 gram brown wool roving

Flexible beading wire

Upholstery or tapestry needle

15 green felt balls, each 1.2 grams

2 crimp beads, #2

Crimping pliers

Wire cutters

Make It

CREATE THE LEAVES

1 Trace the leaf pattern (page 110) onto tracing paper and cut out. Pin the tracing paper pattern to the rayon craft felt, and cut out the felt shape. Repeat for a total of 16 green leaves.

2 Blend the light and dark green roving together (referring to the Techniques section if needed), and then needle felt the blend to both sides of a leaf shape until the total thickness is approximately ¼-inch. Needle felt the remaining leaf shapes in the same manner.

3 Gently wet felt the leaves to smooth out all the holes from the needle felting, and to tighten the fibers. After the final rinse, form the leaf to give it a small arch, and leave to dry.

BUTTON CLOSURE CLASP

4 Roll a .7 gram green felt ball to serve as the closure button. To make the button closure clasp for the necklace, tear off approximately 7 inches of roving, and check the thickness by twisting the two ends in opposite directions. The middle should be approximately ⁷⁄₃₂ inch thick. Double the roving over itself, keeping your index finger in the bottom of the loop. Wet the roving in warm soapy water and begin felting the coil shape, still keeping your index finger in place in order to create a felt loop at the end. Frequently check the loop size against the .7 gram felt ball closure to make sure it fits snugly through the loop. If the loop is too big, the clasp will not serve its purpose. If the loop needs to be smaller, simply remove your finger and felt the coil end a bit more. You can always stretch the loop out a little if it gets too small.

MAKE THE POPPIES

5 To create the flowers, lay out two layers of red roving in an approximate 4-inch diameter. Now tease out the orange roving and lay two thin layers of it on top of the red. Your goal here is to create a blended watercolor effect for the insides of the flowers. Pull off a tuft of yellow roving and create a cobweb that covers the pile. Tear off a small piece of orange roving and add it to the center. Finish off the pile with a cobweb ring of yellow. Remember, there are no rules here; it's simply a matter of personal taste. Keep in

mind that the center of the flower will be covered by a tuft of brown, so plan your layers and spacing accordingly. Turn the pile over onto your wet felting surface so that the yellow side is facedown, and red is faceup. Tear off a small piece of green roving, twirl it into a flat, round dot, and place it onto the back center of the red pile.

6 Wet sand the layers, checking often to make sure the green center piece hasn't slid out of place. If needed, refer back to Making a Flower From a Sheet of Felt, located in the Techniques section.

7 Once you're happy with the shape of your flower, rinse it thoroughly in cool water, towel dry, and reshape.

8 Use the green dot as a guide for the center point, and carefully trim away the unfinished edge so that it's approximately 2 inches from the center of the flower. Remove a little at a time. Re-form the flower, and leave to dry. Repeat for the remaining six flowers.

9 Once the flowers are dry, you can needle felt small tufts of brown roving into the centers. It doesn't take too many pokes with the needle to keep them in place and keep their appearance fluffy versus completely felted.

ASSEMBLE THE NECKLACE

10 Cut the loop end of the button clasp so it's 1½ inches in length. Now set the small green felt ball next to the rest of the remaining green coil and trim off a piece so that, including the felt ball, it equals 1½ inches in length.

11 Thread flexible beading wire through a large upholstery or tapestry needle, and string on a green felt ball. Place two leaves side by side so that they both curl away from each other, and string them on the needle, followed by another large felt ball.

12 Put the needle through the green dot on the back of the poppy and through another large felt ball. Continue stringing this pattern until you have strung the last large green felt ball.

Figure 1

13 Remove the needle and string one crimp bead onto the wire. Replace the needle and string the non-loop green coil piece. If there is an end on the green coil that is thicker, string that end onto the needle first. Then, take a small stitch through the bottom edge of the small felt ball and put the needle back through the green coil. Remove the needle and put the end of the beading wire through the crimp bead (figure 1). Crimp the bead with crimping pliers. Trim away any excess beading wire.

14 Go back through the necklace and adjust each piece, making sure to remove gaps or sections where the pieces fit together too snugly. The goal is for the overall necklace to be able to move freely, but not have any gaps.

Figure 2

15 Trim the beading wire, leaving a 3- to 4-inch tail. String one crimp bead onto the wire. Replace the needle and string the loop end of the clasp, coil end first, onto the needle and then pass the needle back down through the coil (just next to where the wire came up, see figure 2). Remove the needle and put the tail of the wire through the crimp bead. Adjust the tension, and crimp the crimp bead. Trim away the excess wire.

Poppy Ring

What You Need

2 grams red Merino wool

.5 grams orange Merino wool

.5 grams yellow Merion wool

2 grams blended green wool

Felting needle

.1 gram brown wool

Make It

FELT THE RING BAND

1 Make the poppy for the ring just like how they were made for the necklace (steps 5–9), except adjust the overall size of the ring when you trim away the unfinished edge.

2 To make the green band that wraps around your finger, tear off 4 inches of blended green roving. Fold the roving in half, and wet just the middle section of roving; an approximate 1-inch section. Do not wet the whole thing because the sides need to be dry and unfelted when it comes time to needle felt it to the poppy (figure 3). Felt the center section on the work mat as if you were felting a coil. Felt a coil that goes around the bottom of your finger, and up on both sides, but not across the top (figure 4).

ATTACH THE POPPY

3 Once the coil is dry, remove most of the excess loose roving from the coil, but leave enough so that you have something to attach the poppy to.

4 Split one end of the roving in half, wrap it on either side of the green part of the poppy, and needle felt it in place. At this time you may need to remove more excess roving. Remember, if you have too much and it's too bulky, you can always remove the whole coil and start again, making adjustments. Repeat for the opposite side, and finish by needle felting a tuft of brown wool in the center.

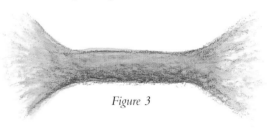

Figure 3

Figure 4

Happy-Go-Lucky Flower Pins

These carefree felt blooms each have their own personalities. Bright hues and starburst petals cut from felt sheets exude a mod Alice in Wonderland attitude. The textured leaves are cut from felted sweaters.

What You Need

3 to 4 grams Merino wool (per flower)

1 to 2 grams of Merino wool (for the inside of the flower)

Cordless sander with felting attachment

Threads for sewing

Seed beads (optional)

Silver button (optional)

Felted green sweater

Pinking shears (optional)

1¼-inch pin back finding

Make It

MAKE A SHEET OF FELT

1 When making a felted flower, I strongly encourage you to try creating new surface textures using novelty fibers, different wools, metallic threads, locks, multiple cob-web layers of wool, and anything else you can dream up. Flowers can be made with just one layer, to stacked flower shapes like the ones featured in the photograph.

2 Lay the wool out on your work mat in a circular square so that the wool measures approximately 5 inches in diameter and three layers thick. Wet felt using a sander, then referring to the Techniques section, make a flower from the sheet of felt.

3 When you're satisfied with the shape, rinse the piece in cool water. At this point you can trim the edge with scissors, or leave it as is. Reshape the flower and leave to dry.

EMBELLISH AND ASSEMBLE THE PIECES

4 The inside petals of the flowers are made by layering smaller flowers and pieces cut from sheets of wool. For example, cutting a small circle out of a thin sheet of felt, and then cutting out notches that point toward the center made the orange sun-like piece. The aqua flower has a small felted red flower, a tiny bit of needle felted coarse wool, golden bead loops, and a flat, brown felted bead. The center is finished off with small stitches drawing the wool down towards the center. Use a few stitches in the middle to hold the layers and pieces together. For the purple flower, I stitched the two felt flowers and the silver button in place with tan embroidery floss, and finished with a knot. Four seed bead clusters of three were stitched on top of the button's holes.

5 Cut the leaves from a felted sweater. See the Techniques section for how to felt a sweater. If you'd like, you can use pinking shears to add a zigzag edge to the leaf. Use a straight stitch to attach the leaves to the back of the flower. Decide the orientation of how you want the flower to be worn, and finish by stitching on the pin back.

Cubed Bracelets

Dense colored cubes are cut from thick felt sheets, and strung together to create bracelets with a clean, minimalist look. Choose your favorite color and intersperse complimenting or contrasting spacer beads.

What You Need

10 grams Merino wool (in a color to match the pearls)

Cordless sander with felting attachment (optional)

Flexible beading wire

Freshwater pearls

Upholstery or tapestry needle

2 crimp beads, #2

Crimping pliers

12mm square toggle clasp

Make It

FELT A SHEET

1 Make a sheet of felt approximately six to eight layers thick. Your raw wool should measure about eight square inches so you'll end up with a piece of felt about four to five inches square. Don't worry if your sheet isn't exact; you're going to cut it up into square beads. Be aware that it'll take a considerable amount of felting to get all the layers to fully felt together; so using a sander will save time and your hands. Don't skimp on felting time or when you cut into the sheet, you're liable to find an un-felted middle.

CUT OUT CUBES

2 Once your sheet of wool has dried, use very sharp scissors to cut it into ¼-inch squares. The easiest way to do this is to cut the wool sheet into ¼-inch wide strips. Then cut the strips into ¼-inch pieces. It's okay if your shapes don't end up exactly square.

STRING THE BEADS

3 Make a kink in the beading wire about one inch from the end so that the needle has a seat. String one pearl onto the beading wire. Slide the needle onto the wire so that it seats in the kink. Carefully twist a square bead onto the needle, making sure that the needle tip goes through the top of the wool versus out through the side. Pliers can assist in pulling the needle and wire through the wool if you experience any difficulty. Continue in this fashion until you have reached your desired length.

4 String one crimp bead followed by one end of the toggle clasp. Bring the tail of the beading wire back through the crimp bead, and crimp. Finish the opposite end of the bracelet in the exact same way with the other end of the toggle clasp. Trim away the excess beading wire.

Three Peas in a Pod

Created in vivid colors and with a fun curled stem, this sweet pea pod
pin lives up to its name. Bubble wrap is folded and taped to make a
hollow mold, allowing felt "peas" to be inserted.

What You Need

12 x 12-inch piece of bubble wrap

Clear packing tape

10 grams green wool roving

2 to 3 grams pink wool roving

1 gram brown Merino wool roving

6-inch long piece of 16-gauge wire
   (rust-proof)

Multipurpose adhesive

Green thread

Round-nose pliers

1-inch pin stem

Make It

CRAFT A FELTING FORM

1 To create a resist (or mold) using bubble wrap and packing tape, cut the bubble wrap into a triangle. To do this, fold the square in half diagonally, and cut along the fold. Roll the triangle up into a snug coil, and secure with a strip of packing tape in the middle. Trim the ends so it resembles a cigar and measures 5½ inches from end to end. It won't look pretty after you cut the ends, but it'll work! Now wrap tape around the ends to secure. To make a bigger or smaller pea pod, simply change the bubble wrap triangle size.

WET FELT AROUND THE FORM

2 Tear a 7-inch length of green wool off the roving, and then split it in half. Add a drop or two of soap to your hands, dip the sliver in some warm soapy water, and begin wrapping evenly around your pod shape, taking care not to twist the roving as you wrap. Always wrap the roving in the same direction, so that there are approximately three to four layers of wool around the pod. See the Techniques section for felting around a form. You can make the inside a different color by wrapping the form first with a wool color of your choosing, followed by the green wool on the outside.

3 Make sure your pod is completely saturated with warm water, but take care not to disturb your layers and wool wrapping. With soapy hands, gently pat the pod shape, rotating it as you work. It's a good idea to rotate the pod in the same direction as you wrapped the wool so as not to undue your work. Continue this for several minutes.

4 You can work the ends of the piece almost like a coil to keep it more tapered. Keep felting the piece until it's just loose around the form. Carefully cut a 1 to 2-inch vertical slit (depending on the length of your pod) down the center, and gently remove the bubble wrap.

5 At this point, use your finger to work the inside of the piece. Check the size of the slit. You can make it a little bigger or leave it alone, depending on how big or how many felt "peas" you want to have. Remember to keep the piece wet. Continue rolling the pod and working the ends until it is fully felted and you have reached the desired size.

FELT THE PEAS AND STEM

6 Roll three or four pink felt balls for the inside of the pod, and set them aside. Divide the brown Merino sliver into ¼ size. Dip a small length into soapy water and wrap it around the 16-gauge wire, taking care not to twist it as you wrap. Add some soap to your fingers and gently smooth over the wool until it is stable enough to roll back and forth on the work mat. Once the wire is felted, rinse in cool water and set aside to dry.

PUTTING IT ALL TOGETHER

7 Place a little bit of adhesive on the inside bottom of the pod and push the felt balls into place. Thread your needle with green thread, and anchor in an inconspicuous place. Draw the two sides of the felt pod in around the pink felt balls by making stitches back and forth, side to side. Try to disguise your stitches by putting the thread in nearly the same place as where you brought it through. Anchor the thread and trim the end.

8 Cut just the tip off one end of the pod, at an angle. This is where the brown felted wire (or stem) will go. Make a small twirl with round-nose pliers at the end of the felted wire. Decide how much of the stem you would like to show, add ½ inch to that measurement, and cut. You can carefully trim a little of the excess brown felt away so that the wire slides down into the pod more easily. Add a drop of glue to the wire, and slide the wire down into the tip of the pod until none of it shows.

9 Finish by stitching a pin back onto the back side of the pea pod.

Templates
SHOWN ACTUAL SIZE

Autumnal Butterfly (page 61)

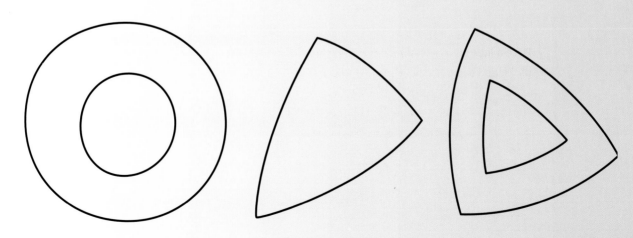

Abstract Brooch Trio (page 90)

Templates
SHOWN ACTUAL SIZE

Flying Heart Brooch (page 72)

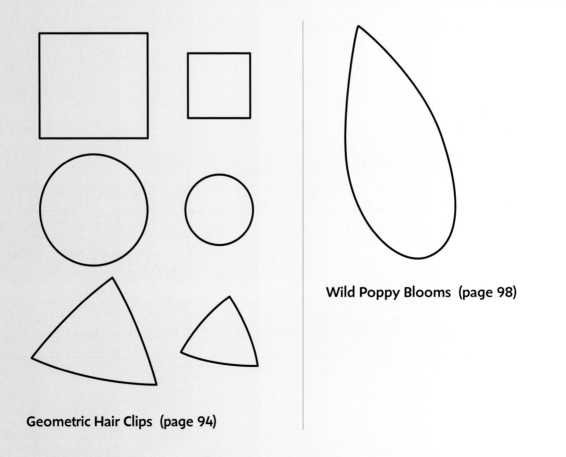

Wild Poppy Blooms (page 98)

Geometric Hair Clips (page 94)

Acknowledgments

Thank you to all the people who made this book possible:

Carol Taylor, president and publisher of Lark Books, and Deborah Morgenthal, vice president and editor-in-chief, for the opportunity to write this book.

To my editor, Linda Kopp, who held my hand throughout this entire project. I will be forever grateful for your enthusiasm, insights, and hard work.

Dana Irwin, art director, for all your creative thinking time that you put into this project. From page layout to photo styling, it all looks great!

Sherrie Hunt, for beautifully photographing my jewelry.

To the artists who shared images of their felt work. You inspire all of us with your amazing talents.

Katie Hacker, dear friend and mentor. Your words of wisdom and encouragement have meant so much to me.

Fellow felting friends in Indiana: Julie Davidson, Patty Baggett, and Matt and Jaime from the Wooly Knob Fiber Mill. I couldn't have asked for better teachers.

My entire family for being the best cheering squad—I can hear you all the way over here in China.

And thank you Butch, my best friend and husband, for supporting me every step of the way with your patience and love.

About the Author

Candie Cooper graduated from Purdue University where she received degrees in fine arts and art education. She's a member of the International Feltmakers Association and the Society of North American Goldsmiths. Candie currently lives in Shenzhen, China, where she works as a studio jeweler and designer. Her passion lies in creating jewelry from mixed materials including but not limited to metal, wool, paper, and wood. Her jewelry has been exhibited throughout the United States, England, and Europe.

Index